At Issue

Is the Western Diet Making the World Sick?

Other Books in the At Issue Series:

At Issue

Is the Western Diet Making the World Sick?

Susan Hunnicutt, Book Editor

GREENHAVEN PRESS
A part of Gale, Cengage Learning

 GALE
CENGAGE Learning·

Detroit • New York • San Francisco • New Haven, Conn • Waterville, Maine • London

GALE
CENGAGE Learning·

Elizabeth Des Chenes, *Director, Publishing Solutions*

© 2013 Greenhaven Press, a part of Gale, Cengage Learning

Gale and Greenhaven Press are registered trademarks used herein under license.

For more information, contact:
Greenhaven Press
27500 Drake Rd.
Farmington Hills, MI 48331-3535
Or you can visit our Internet site at gale.cengage.com

For product information and technology assistance, contact us at

Gale Customer Support, 1-800-877-4253
For permission to use material from this text or product, submit all requests online at www.cengage.com/permissions

Further permissions questions can be emailed to permissionrequest@cengage.com

Articles in Greenhaven Press anthologies are often edited for length to meet page requirements. In addition, original titles of these works are changed to clearly present the main thesis and to explicitly indicate the author's opinion. Every effort is made to ensure that Greenhaven Press accurately reflects the original intent of the authors. Every effort has been made to trace the owners of copyrighted material.

Cover image © Images.com/Corbis.

LIBRARY OF CONGRESS CATALOGING-IN-PUBLICATION DATA

Is the Western diet making the world sick? / Susan Hunnicutt, book editor.
    p. cm. -- (At issue)
  Includes bibliographical references and index.
  ISBN 978-0-7377-6191-7 (hardcover) -- ISBN 978-0-7377-6192-4 (pbk.)
  1. Diet--Standards--United States. 2. Nutrition--Social aspects. 3. Health--United
States. I. Hunnicutt, Susan.
  RA784.I59 2013
  613.2--dc23
                                                                    2012033954

Printed in the United States of America
1 2 3 4 5 6 7 16 15 14 13 12

Contents

Introduction

According to the Centers for Disease Control and Prevention (CDC), chronic diseases like heart disease, stroke, cancer, and diabetes are among the most common, costly, and preventable of health problems in the United States, affecting one in every two adults. Heart disease, cancer, and stroke account for more than 50 percent of deaths each year, and diabetes, which can result in kidney failure, loss of limbs, and blindness, is the leading cause of disability among adults.

Poor nutrition has been identified as a major factor in the high incidence of all of these conditions. Recently, attention has focused on shortcomings of the so-called Western diet; this diet has been shaped by a series of agricultural innovations that began during the Neolithic period and has continued to the modern era with the development of food-manufacturing systems associated with industrial agriculture. In the typical US or Western diet, some nutrition experts claim, 72 percent of energy value is provided by foods that were not part of the diets of hominids, early humans, or close human ancestors. These include dairy products (10 percent of energy value in today's typical diet), cereal grains (23.9 percent of energy value), refined sugars (18.6 percent of energy value), refined vegetable oils (17.6 percent of energy value), and alcohol (1.4 percent of energy value). Often these foods are presented in mixtures, for example in cookies, cakes, crackers, chips, snack foods, and pizza, all of which can be combinations of processed sugars, fats, dairy products, and grains. Processed sugars also appear in large quantities in soft drinks, candy, and ice cream.

According to an article published in 2005 in the *American Journal of Clinical Nutrition*, the problem with the Western diet is that the pace of dietary innovations has outdistanced the ability of the human species to make adaptive physiological changes. Significant health-related differences that distinguish the Western diet from the diets of early humans and other hominids include glycemic load, fatty acid composition, macronutrient composition, micronutrient density, acid-base balance, sodium-potassium ratio, and fiber content. As explained in the article, "The evolutionary collision of our ancient genome with the nutritional qualities of recently introduced foods may underlie many of the chronic diseases of Western civilization."

The media, following the lead of the biomedical research community, have largely adopted the use of the term "Western diet" to refer to a diet that is high in saturated fats and carbohydrates of poor quality, and lacking in higher quality carbohydrates—such as fresh fruits, vegetables, and whole grains—and proteins such as those found in seafood and poultry. The following headlines are representative: "Cancer Risk Higher with Western Diet" (*USA Today*, July 11, 2007); "'Western' Diet Is a Global Heart Risk" (*CBS News*, October 20, 2008); "Western Diet Pattern 'Promotes Metabolic Syndrome'" (*Dairy Reporter*, February 8, 2008); and "Western Diet Populates Kids' Stomachs with Bad Bacteria" (*Business Week*, August 2, 2010).

Despite its widespread and persistent use in the media, the Western diet label has recently drawn criticism for being imprecise and misleading. In April 2011, for example, the creators of The Spartan Diet posted an article on their website entitled "Stop Calling It the 'Western Diet'!" Use of the term is convenient, authors Amira Elgan and Mike Elgan complain, but it's not accurate. "When people say 'Western Diet,' they're really talking about an industrial diet—the factory foods developed since the Industrial revolution, which became far more pervasive since the end of World War II. Processed foods, stripped of nutrients and loaded down with added fat, artificial colors, preservatives, sugar, corn syrup and all the rest—these concepts are recent inventions and as alien to the Western tradition as chopsticks."

In keeping with academic conventions, the Elgans argue that the term "Western diet" should be reserved for culinary traditions that can be traced to ancient Greece and its cultural descendants. For example, olive oil, red wine, and pomegranates, widely recognized for their healthful qualities, are all technically Western. Other healthful foods associated with agricultural and culinary traditions that are rooted in the West include figs, apples, pears, grapes, lettuce, cabbage, peas, beans, whole grain wheat and barley, almonds, walnuts, onions, and garlic.

According to the Elgans, one problem with the prevailing use of the term "Western diet" is the implication that "Eastern" cuisines are to be preferred. The white rice that is featured in many contemporary Asian cuisines is not significantly different from white bread, they point out, and many Eastern cultures offer sauces that are high in unhealthy carbohydrates and fats. "You can find industrialized junk food versions of both 'Eastern' and 'Western' foods all over the world," they note, citing ramen noodles in a Styrofoam cup as just one example. "It's absurd to use the word 'Western' to identify the diet that's wrecking modern health. . . . The real villain is industrial food. And the solution is to reject such foods and embrace the traditionally prepared healthiest foods from all over the world, including and perhaps especially from the West."

As this discussion shows, issues that have emerged in the ongoing conversation about the so-called Western diet point to significant recent changes in the way the scientific community thinks about nutritional value as well as dietary dangers, and also to the widespread perception of a growing, diet-related global health crisis. Commentators debate whether industrial agriculture and the modern food industry are largely responsible for the crisis, or whether there are other factors, rooted in the agricultural innovations of the distant human past, that must also be considered. Other discussions revolve around the role poverty plays in limiting access to nutritious foods and whether it is helpful to designate certain areas as food deserts, or if that language hinders the development of local, non-industrial food producers. These and many other issues are considered in *At Issue: Is the Western Diet Making the World Sick?*

1

Poverty Is a Major Factor Contributing to Obesity and Poor Health

Daniel Engber

Daniel Engber is a senior editor at Slate.

Advocates for universal health coverage often state that reducing obesity will result in health savings on a national level. However, studies show that obesity, poverty, and illness are related in complex ways. To improve public health, it may be more effective to focus on reducing poverty than to aim interventions directly at reducing obesity.

In my last column ("Let Them Drink Water!"), I suggested that a tax on sweetened soft drinks would move the nation toward an apartheid of pleasure in which the poor must drink from the faucet while the rich enjoy superpremium fruit juice. I also argued that the soda tax discriminates on economic grounds, since rates of soft drink consumption tend to be highest in poor, nonwhite communities. But supporters of the measure counter that these very communities would benefit most from drinking less soda and that revenue from a regressive fat tax could be spent on laudable progressive goals—like universal health care.

Poverty and Obesity Tend to Overlap

The relationship between poverty and obesity keeps turning up in the debate over health care reform. Among the 46 million people in America who lack medical insurance, about two-thirds earn less than twice the poverty level. Advocates for universal coverage say that we can pay for all these new patients by cutting back on obesity rates, since excess fat accounts for 9 percent of the country's spending on medical care. (During the campaign, then-Sen. Obama claimed this might save the Medicare system $1 trillion.) Some even suggest that a reform package should include special taxes or higher premiums for fat people. That idea starts to seem misguided, though, when you consider that poverty and obesity tend to overlap in some complicated ways.

We know . . . that the lower your income, the more likely you are to inhabit an "obesogenic" environment. Food options in poor neighborhoods are severely limited.

As a matter of public health, it might be more important to help poor people than fat people. According to epidemiologist Peter Muennig, the relative risk of mortality for being obese is between 1 and 2. That means that, controlling for other factors, someone who's really fat is up to twice as likely to die early as someone whose body mass index is in the normal range. But if you compare people from the top and bottom of the wage scale (with everything else held constant), the risk ratio goes up to about 3.5. In other words, it's much better for your health to be rich and fat than poor and thin.

Those in greatest need, furthermore, tend to be both poor *and* fat. We know, for instance, that the lower your income, the more likely you are to inhabit an "obesogenic" environment. Food options in poor neighborhoods are severely limited: It's a lot easier to find quarter waters and pork rinds on the corner than fresh fruit and vegetables. Low-income workers may also have less time to cook their own meals, less money to join sports clubs, and less opportunity to exercise outdoors.

Anyone who's fat is more likely to be poor and sick. Anyone who's poor is more likely to be fat and sick. And anyone who's sick is more likely to be poor and fat.

If poverty can be fattening, so, too, can fat be impoverishing. Paul Ernsberger, a professor of nutrition at Case Western Reserve University, lays out this argument in an essay from *The Fat Studies Reader*. . . . Women who are two standard deviations overweight (that's 64 pounds above normal) make 9 percent less money, which equates to having 1.5 fewer years of education or three fewer years of work experience. Obese women are also half as likely to attend college as their peers and 20 percent less likely to get married. (Marriage seems to help alleviate poverty.)

When it comes to public health, the relationship between poverty and obesity gets more convoluted. Being fat can make you poor, and being poor can make you sick, which means that being fat can make you sick irrespective of any weight-related diseases. Fatness (or the lifestyle associated with obesity) also creates its own health problems, regardless of how much money you have—and health problems tend to make people poor, through hospital bills and missed days of work. So fat can be impoverishing irrespective of any weight-related discrimination.

A Dense Web of Interlinked Causes

The point here is that sickness, poverty, and obesity are spun together in a dense web of reciprocal causality. Anyone who's fat is more likely to be poor and sick. Anyone who's poor is more likely to be fat and sick. And anyone who's sick is more likely to be poor and fat.

Sociologists describe these patterns in terms of social gradients. The "health-wealth gradient" refers to the fact that, as a general rule, the richer you are, the healthier you are. This applies across different countries and across the full range of social classes within the same country. (It's not just that the very poorest people are sick.) No one knows exactly what causes the health-wealth gradient or why it's so resilient. It may be that rich people have access to better health care. Or, as we've seen, it could be that being sick costs you money. Then there's the possibility that poor people have a greater incentive to behave in unhealthy ways: Since they don't have as much money to spend on happiness, they "spend" their health instead. (The pleasures of smoking and eating, for example, are easy on the wallet and hard on the body.)

If we spread around the wealth a little better, poor people would end up healthier—and thinner—than they were before.

Related to the health-wealth gradient is what we might call the "girth-wealth" gradient. In 1989, a pair of researchers named Albert Stunkard and Jeffery Sobal pored over several decades' worth of data on obesity rates and concluded that socioeconomic status and body size were inversely related among women in developed countries. A recent review by Lindsay McLaren found that the pattern of poor women being fatter than rich ones has begun to spread into the developing world. (For men, the girth-wealth gradient tends to go in the opposite direction, and the health effects of obesity are somewhat diminished.)

Both gradients appear to be deeply entrenched in modern life, and we shouldn't count on universal health coverage to erase either one. International surveys suggest that the development of free medical care—through the National Health Service in the United Kingdom, for example—doesn't much alter the fundamental relationship between health and wealth. It's also not clear that expanded health coverage is likely to make the poor any less fat. A study published over the summer [2009] even suggests that the opposite might be true—a public option could end up increasing obesity rates among the newly insured.

The mere existence of these gradients does suggest that if we spread around the wealth a little better, poor people would end up healthier—and thinner—than they were before. According to British economists Richard Wilkinson and Kate Pickett, this benefit wouldn't necessarily come at the expense of the rich. Their new book, *The Spirit Level: Why Greater Equality Makes Societies Stronger*, uses data from the World Bank, the World Health Organization, and the U.S. Census to argue that disparities in income produce a wide range of social ills—like obesity, teen pregnancy, mental illness, murder, and infant mortality—that could be addressed by shrinking the gap between the haves and the have-nots. Indeed, the United Kingdom's Labor government has taken up this charge in recent years, with a series of measures to reduce inequality in the name of public health.

A Possible Solution: Invest in Education

The United States could try to do the same, by raising the minimum wage or increasing earned-income tax credits. In 2001, Princeton economist Angus Deaton considered the implications of a Robin Hood health policy. . . . Deaton concluded that a direct redistribution of wealth might be an efficient way to improve the health of the poorest Americans. But he warned that equality shouldn't be treated as an end in itself. A fancy new treatment, for example, might steepen the health-wealth gradient when it's first introduced, since only the rich can afford it. But that doesn't mean we should avoid medical breakthroughs for the sake of public health. According to Deaton, a saner approach would be to invest in education, since better schooling seems to improve your health and raise your income, too.

You don't hear anyone suggesting that better schools could pay for health care reform, though. Instead, we've pegged our hopes on a national weight-loss regime—a redistribution of girth instead of wealth. If being poor can make you fat and vice versa, then we can't solve one health problem while ignoring the other. Yet we act as though the war on obesity can be separated out from the war on poverty: Consider the soda tax—an anti-obesity measure that shifts money *away from the poor.*

Why are we so fixated on body size? Another social gradient might be playing out in this policy debate: It turns out that the richer you are, the more likely you are to be on a diet. (Among fat people, more wealth correlates with lower self-esteem.) So it's only natural that we'd be hung up on the issue of obesity—we're projecting.

2

Lifestyle Diseases Are Increasing in the Developing World

Felicity Lawrence

Felicity Lawrence is a special correspondent for the Guardian *newspaper. She has written two bestselling books on the food business,* Not on the Label *and* Eat Your Heart Out.

Developing countries are the newest market for multinational food and beverage corporations, and greater access to highly processed food and drinks is leading to an epidemic of so-called lifestyle diseases, such as diabetes, heart disease, and alcoholism, in these countries. Processed foods tend to be less expensive and appear to be more convenient than healthier foods, such as fresh produce, leading impoverished people to make poor choices. Increasingly, malnutrition is occurring side-by-side with obesity. In 2008, nearly two-thirds of all deaths worldwide were attributed to lifestyle diseases.

Nestlé is using a floating supermarket to take its products to remote communities in the Amazon. Unilever has a small army of door-to-door vendors selling to low-income villages in India and west and east Africa. The brewer SABMiller has developed cheap beers in some African countries as part of a "price ladder" to its premium lager brands, and, as a leading Coca-Cola bottler and distributor, is aiming to double fizzy drinks sales in South African townships.

As affluent western markets reach saturation point, global food and drink firms have been opening up new frontiers among people living on $2 a day in low- and middle-income countries. The world's poor have become their vehicle for growth.

The companies say they are finding innovative ways to give isolated people the kind of choices the rich have enjoyed for years and are providing valuable jobs and incomes to some of the most marginalised. But health campaigners are raising the alarm. They fear the arrival of highly processed food and drink is also a vector for the lifestyle diseases, such as obesity, diabetes, heart disease and alcoholism, which are increasing at unprecedented rates in developing countries.

We have this kind of "hidden hunger" . . . where it's easy to fill the hole in one's belly with low-nutrient, cheap, empty-calorie foods . . . but not meet the body's long-term nutritional needs.

Health Budgets Cannot Keep Up

The South African minister of health, Aaron Motsoaledi, gives a grim interpretation of what that means for his country when he spoke to the *Guardian* earlier this month [November 2011]. "Health budgets will break because of the cost of amputations, artificial limbs, wheelchairs and cardiac surgery."

A UN summit in New York in September confirmed the scale of the health crisis. Nearly two-thirds of all deaths worldwide in 2008 were attributable to lifestyle diseases. By 2030 these non-communicable diseases (NCDs) are expected to be the cause of nearly five times as many deaths as the traditional, infectious scourges of poor nations such as TB, malaria and AIDS.

Last year 39% of acquisition deals by consumer goods companies were in emerging markets, compared with just 1% in 2008, according to the Grocer's OC&C Global 50 league table.

As diets and lifestyles in developing countries change, their patterns of disease are following those seen in industrialised countries in the north equally rapidly. But for poor countries there is a double whammy: they have started suffering from high rates of NCDs before they have managed to deal with hunger and malnutrition. The double burden is devastating both their economic growth and their health budgets.

In South Africa, about a quarter of schoolchildren are now obese or overweight, as are 60% of women and 31% of men. Diabetes rates are soaring. Yet, nearly 20% of children aged one to nine have stunted growth, having suffered the kind of long-term malnutrition that leaves irreversible damage.

Moreover, obesity and malnutrition often occur in the same household, according to Leonie Joubert, a researcher at the University of Cape Town's centre of criminology, and author of a forthcoming book on food security. "It's not a case of having massive starvation on one end of the spectrum, and gluttony on the other. We have this kind of 'hidden hunger', almost pervasive in poorer communities where it's easy to fill the hole in one's belly with low-nutrient, cheap, empty-calorie foods to satisfy one's hunger now, but not meet the body's long-term nutritional needs."

Dr Motsoaledi is a medically trained former anti-apartheid activist, and does not shy away from the dramatic. He marked the day the 7 billionth child was thought to have been born in to the global population by scrubbing up and delivering a baby himself by caesarean section. He then tied the new mother's tubes as his contribution to family planning.

Taking Radical Action

Pushing through radical action on NCDs is one of his priorities. He said: "When I was a medical student under apartheid, heart attacks were a rare thing for black people. The main illnesses then were TB, malaria and kwashiorkor [malnutrition from protein deficiency]. That's no longer true. Africans are eating more and more junk processed foods instead of their traditional diet. My mother hardly went to the shop. Anything you wanted to eat you grew and took straight from the soil. We had free range chickens, vegetables. I used to walk a long distance to school. My children hardly walk a metre from the car. Children are put in front of the TV and they eat junk in front of it. It is not a life of activity. It's a globalised world; we can't expect to be left untouched."

He wants to curb the marketing of tobacco and alcohol and regulate junk food, starting with reducing salt in bread and eliminating trans fats, but he anticipates a fight. "There's going to be war over this next year."

"It is like climate change. Are we going to do something about it when we are looking down the barrel of a gun and it is at its worst, when budgets have become unmanageable because of the sheer weight of disease? If those of us in power don't do something now, that is what will happen. Anybody who dilly dallies on non-communicable diseases will be forced to act when the situation is out of control."

The main obstacle to action was profit. "Industry is resisting very strongly, of course. The only reason people are not doing enough is the bottom dollar."

Governments trying to restrict the marketing activity have found themselves challenged in court. Motsoaledi is watching the case brought by the tobacco industry against the Australian government, which wants to ban all branding on cigarette packs. "I want a similar structure for alcohol control," he says.

He knows that he is likely to be the target of determined lobbying as well as legal action.

Powerful Interests Will Defend Themselves

Unlike the UK secretary of state for health, who has invited food and alcohol companies to join his "responsibility deals" on public health, Motsoaledi sees no place for industry in helping draw up policy. "You cannot make policy with them, they will just shape it for their profits. You can't sit in the same room with a national brewer and come up with a policy on alcohol to benefit the nation." The interests Motsoaledi is taking on are indeed powerful and quick to defend themselves. SABMiller, the largest brewer in South Africa, points out in documents on its "alcohol responsibility" web pages that it supports 3% of the total employment in South Africa, and generates taxes—mostly from excise duty on its products—that account for 5% of the government's tax revenue. It believes industry can play a role in tackling health problems and argues that its marketing promotes brand loyalty, not greater drinking. Kristin Wolfe, head of alcohol policy at SAB-Miller, said: "We market to our target consumer; we don't go after non-drinkers. What the UN wanted in New York was a whole societal approach. Marketing is seen as just one factor. It has to be responsible, but there's a distinction between harmful drinking and marketing. It's a more enlightened approach to get industry to do what it can; we will make better progress." The company points to its investment in projects to tackle alcohol harm and bring unlicensed outlets within regulation.

Being thin and losing weight is associated with AIDS and TB, which makes being overweight seem more acceptable.

Thandi Puoane, a professor at University of Western Cape, has tracked the increase in NCDs since the end of apartheid. With sanctions lifted and freedom of movement introduced after the multiracial elections in 1994, there was a rapid change in the profile of disease. Large numbers of black people have moved from rural areas where they had to walk miles for water and fuel to the townships on the edge of the cities. The townships are overcrowded, unemployment is high and infrastructure, such as electricity and sanitation, poor or nonexistent. Fast-food outlets and imports of processed foods proliferated after markets re-opened.

Large numbers of people moved to townships, where infrastructure is poor.

"People coming here buy fatty, sugary food and drink because it's cheap and it feels a luxury not to cook," Puoane said. "Cooking fuel is expensive. They can buy from street vendors on credit. Fear of crime, often fuelled by alcohol, stops them taking exercise. They think they are happy because they are fat and when they go back to their rural areas people say, 'you must be doing well, you have put on weight.'" Being thin and losing weight is associated with AIDS and TB, which makes being overweight seem more acceptable.

Every other shack shop, and even a church hall, is adorned with Coca-Cola branding. Retail giants have arrived, and Walmart has just taken over one of the large South African chains.

Opening Health Clubs

Khayelitsha, a township that sprawls for miles alongside the highway from Cape Town to the Cape flats, is one of the largest and fastest growing in South Africa. Unofficial estimates put its population at a million. Here you can see the crisis of obesity and other NCDs writ large. Unemployment is nearly 60%, and 70% of residents live in shacks with no running water. Alcohol use and violent crime are high and many people are overweight, particularly among women and teenage girls.

The faculty of public health at the university has pioneered health clubs to address the problem.

Lungiswa Tsolekile, a dietitian working on the health project, described some of the cultural barriers to being healthy in this environment, as she took me on a tour. She said access to affordable fresh food was limited. Street stalls sold cheap but often fatty foods, such as the chicken skin discarded by poultry factories, or chicken feet, tripe and sheep's heads. Processed soup, often high in salt, is popular as a cheap gravy to go with the staple of maize porridge. Every other shack shop, and even a church hall, is adorned with Coca-Cola branding. Retail giants have arrived, and Walmart has just taken over one of the large South African chains, but a taxi to the nearest supermarket for fresh fruit and vegetables costs four rand, more than many can spare. She pointed out the numerous billboards advertising alcohol, too.

The ShopRite supermarket we visited was packed with people pushing basket-sized trolleys—the average spend here is small by European standards. There was fresh food available, but a kilo of tomatoes cost more than a 2-litre bottle of cola. At the entrance to the store, leaflets were promoting cut-price alcohol with free mobile phone deals; the aisle ends had special offers for Nestlé's coffee-style caffeine drink Ricoffy listing dextrin (a starch sugar) and dextrose (a form of sugar) as its two main ingredients, and Nestlé's Cremora, a coffee creamer whose principle ingredients are glucose syrup solids and palm fat. The checkout was stacked with sweets alongside "funeral plan pay-as-you-go" starter packs.

Nestlé's floating supermarket took its maiden voyage on the Amazon last year and has been distributing its products to around 800,000 isolated riverside people each month ever since.

"We use physical exercise in the health clubs as a vehicle to help with other aspects of health, including cooking sessions on how to prepare healthy food with traditional ingredients. We pick up a lot of hypertension, high blood glucose and diabetes," Tsolekile said.

Nestlé meanwhile sees itself as "providing products that are healthier, safe and affordable for consumers wherever they are". It says it gives consumers the information they need to make healthier choices, through the labelling and sponsored education programmes. "Often in emerging markets, processed food appeals to consumers because it is guaranteed to be safe. It can also help address deficiencies. We fortify many of what we call our popularly positioned products to help meet this need," a Nestlé spokesman said. "Our range of products in South Africa and in Brazil is wider than that offered by many of our competitors. We are always looking for ways to improve both the taste and nutritional value of our products."

Unilever believes its door-to-door sales network has helped lift people out of poverty. Trevor Gorin, its global media relations director, said: "It has essentially empowered people in rural communities, largely women, to become entrepreneurs, generating income—with all the concomitant benefits this income generates. Most of the Unilever products sold through it are home and personal care products to improve sanitation and personal hygiene. The food products are usually things like stock cubes and tea."

A Floating Supermarket

Nestlé's floating supermarket took its maiden voyage on the Amazon last year and has been distributing its products to around 800,000 isolated riverside people each month ever since. Christened Nestlé Até Você, Nestle comes to you, the boat carries around 300 branded processed lines, including ice creams, and infant milk, but no other foods. The products are in smaller pack sizes to make them more affordable. The boat also acts as a collection point for the network of door-to-door saleswomen Nestlé has recruited to promote its brands. Targeting consumers from socioeconomic classes C, D and E is part of the company's strategic plan for growth, it says. Nestlé has also set up a network of more than 7,500 resellers and 220 microdistributors to reach those at the bottom of the pyramid in the slums of Rio and São Paulo and other major Brazilian cities.

3

American Agribusiness Promotes Diabetes and Other Chronic Diseases

Michael Pollan

Michael Pollan, a professor of journalism at the University of California, Berkeley, is the author of several books, including The Omnivore's Dilemma, In Defense of Food: An Eater's Manifesto, *and* Food Rules: An Eater's Manual.

Success in bringing health-care costs under control is a major goal of US health-care reform. To the extent that the United States subsidizes the "Western diet," it is contributing to current high levels of heart disease, Type 2 diabetes, and other chronic conditions that are associated with the consumption of highly processed and "cheap" foods. The major step to improving Americans' health will not be the health-care reform bill but reform of the country's food system. Health insurers may actually lead this fight, once they can no longer turn away people with pre-existing conditions, such as diabetes, and have to incur the true costs of America's addiction to processed and cheap foods.

To listen to President Obama ... or to just about anyone else in the health care debate, you would think that the biggest problem with health care in America is the system itself—perverse incentives, inefficiencies, unnecessary tests and procedures, lack of competition, and greed.

No one disputes that the $2.3 trillion we devote to the health care industry is often spent unwisely, but the fact that the United States spends twice as much per person as most European countries on health care can be substantially explained, as a study released last month [August 2009] says, by our being fatter. Even the most efficient health care system that the administration could hope to devise would still confront a rising tide of chronic disease linked to diet.

We're spending $147 billion to treat obesity, $116 billion to treat diabetes, and hundreds of billions more to treat cardiovascular disease and the many types of cancer that have been linked to the so-called Western diet.

The Costs of Being Fat

That's why our success in bringing health care costs under control ultimately depends on whether Washington can summon the political will to take on and reform a second, even more powerful industry: the food industry.

According to the Centers for Disease Control and Prevention, three-quarters of health care spending now goes to treat "preventable chronic diseases." Not all of these diseases are linked to diet—there's smoking, for instance—but many, if not most, of them are.

We're spending $147 billion to treat obesity, $116 billion to treat diabetes, and hundreds of billions more to treat cardiovascular disease and the many types of cancer that have been linked to the so-called Western diet. One recent study estimated that 30 percent of the increase in health care spending over the past 20 years could be attributed to the soaring rate of obesity, a condition that now accounts for nearly a tenth of all spending on health care.

The American way of eating has become the elephant in the room in the debate over health care. The president has made a few notable allusions to it, and, by planting her vegetable garden on the South Lawn, Michelle Obama has tried to focus our attention on it. Just last month, Mr. Obama talked about putting a farmers' market in front of the White House, and building new distribution networks to connect local farmers to public schools so that student lunches might offer more fresh produce and fewer Tater Tots. He's even floated the idea of taxing soda.

The Difficulty of Reforming the Food Industry

But so far, food system reform has not figured in the national conversation about health care reform. And so the government is poised to go on encouraging America's fast-food diet with its farm policies even as it takes on added responsibilities for covering the medical costs of that diet. To put it more bluntly, the government is putting itself in the uncomfortable position of subsidizing both the costs of treating Type 2 diabetes and the consumption of high-fructose corn syrup.

There's more money in amputating the limbs of diabetics than in counseling them on diet and exercise.

Why the disconnect? Probably because reforming the food system is politically even more difficult than reforming the health care system. At least in the health care battle, the administration can count some powerful corporate interests on its side—like the large segment of the Fortune 500 that has concluded the current system is unsustainable.

That is hardly the case when it comes to challenging agribusiness. Cheap food is going to be popular as long as the social and environmental costs of that food are charged to the future. There's lots of money to be made selling fast food and then treating the diseases that fast food causes. One of the leading products of the American food industry has become patients for the American health care industry.

The market for prescription drugs and medical devices to manage Type 2 diabetes, which the Centers for Disease Control estimates will afflict one in three Americans born after 2000, is one of the brighter spots in the American economy. As things stand, the health care industry finds it more profitable to treat chronic diseases than to prevent them. There's more money in amputating the limbs of diabetics than in counseling them on diet and exercise.

As for the insurers, you would think preventing chronic diseases would be good business, but, at least under the current rules, it's much better business simply to keep patients at risk for chronic disease out of your pool of customers, whether through lifetime caps on coverage or rules against pre-existing conditions or by figuring out ways to toss patients overboard when they become ill.

The Rules May Change Soon

But these rules may well be about to change—and, when it comes to reforming the American diet and food system, that step alone could be a game changer. Even under the weaker versions of health care reform now on offer, health insurers would be required to take everyone at the same rates, provide a standard level of coverage and keep people on their rolls regardless of their health. Terms like "pre-existing conditions" and "underwriting" would vanish from the health insurance rulebook—and, when they do, the relationship between the health insurance industry and the food industry will undergo a sea change.

The moment these new rules take effect, health insurance companies will promptly discover they have a powerful interest in reducing rates of obesity and chronic diseases linked to diet. A patient with Type 2 diabetes incurs additional health care costs of more than $6,600 a year; over a lifetime, that can come to more than $400,000. Insurers will quickly figure out that every case of Type 2 diabetes they can prevent adds $400,000 to their bottom line. Suddenly, every can of soda or Happy Meal or chicken nugget on a school lunch menu will look like a threat to future profits.

Few things could do more to slow the rise of Type 2 diabetes among adolescents than to reduce their soda consumption, which represents 15 percent of their caloric intake.

When health insurers can no longer evade much of the cost of treating the collateral damage of the American diet, the movement to reform the food system—everything from farm policy to food marketing and school lunches—will acquire a powerful and wealthy ally, something it hasn't really ever had before.

The Health Insurers Will Take on Agribusiness

Agribusiness dominates the agriculture committees of Congress, and has swatted away most efforts at reform. But what happens when the health insurance industry realizes that our system of farm subsidies makes junk food cheap, and fresh produce dear, and thus contributes to obesity and Type 2 diabetes? It will promptly get involved in the fight over the farm bill—which is to say, the industry will begin buying seats on those agriculture committees and demanding that the next bill be written with the interests of the public health more firmly in mind.

In the same way much of the health insurance industry threw its weight behind the campaign against smoking, we can expect it to support, and perhaps even help pay for, public education efforts like New York City's bold new ad campaign against drinking soda. At the moment, a federal campaign to discourage the consumption of sweetened soft drinks is a political nonstarter, but few things could do more to slow the rise of Type 2 diabetes among adolescents than to reduce their soda consumption, which represents 15 percent of their caloric intake.

That's why it's easy to imagine the industry throwing its weight behind a soda tax. School lunch reform would become its cause, too, and in time the industry would come to see that the development of regional food systems, which make fresh produce more available and reduce dependence on heavily processed food from far away, could help prevent chronic disease and reduce their costs.

Recently a team of designers from M.I.T. and Columbia was asked by the foundation of the insurer UnitedHealthcare to develop an innovative systems approach to tackling childhood obesity in America. Their conclusion surprised the designers as much as their sponsor: they determined that promoting the concept of a "foodshed"—a diversified, regional food economy—could be the key to improving the American diet.

All of which suggests that passing a health care reform bill, no matter how ambitious, is only the first step in solving our health care crisis. To keep from bankrupting ourselves, we will then have to get to work on improving our health— which means going to work on the American way of eating.

But even if we get a health care bill that does little more than require insurers to cover everyone on the same basis, it could put us on that course.

For it will force the industry, and the government, to take a good hard look at the elephant in the room and galvanize a movement to slim it down.

4

Industrialized Agriculture Has Produced an Unhealthy Food System

David Wallinga

David Wallinga is a physician and senior advisor in Science, Food and Health at the Institute for Agriculture and Trade Policy. He founded Healthy Food Action, a national network of health professionals, including physicians, to advocate for a future where health is at the center of the American food and farming system.

Physicians have an important role to play in educating the public about food-related crises that are impacting the health-care system. In addition to obesity, problems like food-borne illnesses, toxins, and pollutants in the food supply are all having an impact on health and health-care costs. These problems are the result of an industrial food system that values only production, without concern for the healthfulness of its products or for the environment in which they are produced. It is important for physicians to become actively involved in building a healthier food system.

Food-related crises are reverberating through our health care system. It's time for physicians to not simply treat the fallout but to help get to the root of the problem and prevent it.

David Wallinga, "An Unhealthy Food System: Suggestions for Physician Advocacy," *San Francisco Medicine*, November, 2010. Copyright © 2010 by San Francisco Medicine. All rights reserved. Reproduced by permission.

Obesity is an expensive plague, costing at least $147 billion per year just in direct treatment costs. Costs of managing the related diseases would push the total higher. But the problems only begin with the obesity epidemic. We face near-continuous outbreaks of food-borne disease: salmonella in eggs this year [2010], a different salmonella strain (*S. typhimurium DT104*) in Colorado ground beef and in peanut butter last year, and so on. Food safety threats have always been present. What is new are mammoth food plants that amass huge quantities of meat or another product from so many locations, mix it, and then send it all across the country—factors making national disease outbreaks more likely and more difficult to track back to the source. The hamburger felling one particular young dancer with *E. coli 0157.H7*, according to the *New York Times*, had ingredients from probably tens of different cows and from slaughterhouses in Nebraska, Texas, and Uruguay. Another 10 percent of that burger came from trimmed beef fat from who-knows-how-many cows collected by Beef Products, Inc., a South Dakota company, which after collection douses the trimmings with ammonia to kill the *E. coli*.

The health of the food we put in our mouths cannot be divorced from the health of the natural world, the "agro-ecosystem" that gives rise to it.

Arsenic and Antibiotics Are Routinely Used

Then there are problems with arsenic and antibiotics. Both are put routinely into feed for healthy animals. Both are unnecessary practices, as neither European meat producers nor American organic producers use them. This overuse of human antibiotics (tetracycline, penicillin, erythromycins, streptogramins, etc.) helps create bacterial resistance transmitted to humans. Leadership of the Food and Drug Administration (FDA) and the Centers for Disease Control and Prevention (CDC) acknowledge the routine use of medically important antibiotics in animal feed as a significant public health problem, and one that has to change.

Arsenic and antibiotics given to animals inevitably end up in manure, and thereby in the broader environment, where they help create environmental reservoirs of resistant bacteria. They are just two of a greater number of pollutants arising from industrialized agriculture that wend their way into water supplies. Many others, like atrazine and other common pesticides, are endocrine disrupters—chemicals that disrupt hormone synthesis or function. Other food-chain pollutants of note include food dyes that now appear to worsen hyperactivity, mixtures of pesticides common on produce, and hormone-disrupting bisphenol A (BPA) in baby bottles and the plastic liners of infant formula cans. Last year, we coauthored two papers pulling the curtain off the problem of mercury in high fructose corn syrup. Caustic soda from one particular kind of chemical factory is mercury-contaminated and intentionally used in making this sweetener that's put into so many foods for children and others. The list goes on.

The Problem of Industrialization

It's important to not simply consider the litany of food system problems as isolated incidents. Rather, these crises are interrelated. And the systemic or interrelated nature of these problems cries out for health professionals to stand up and be a voice for change to a healthier food system.

Food system crises are related precisely because it is a system. (By the food system, I mean the totality of food production, but also its harvest, processing, marketing, and distribution.) The hallmark of any system—like the human body—is that it is dynamic and functions as a complex whole, making it impossible to easily divorce one part of the system from any other. Thus, the health of the food we put in our mouths cannot be divorced from the health of the natural world, the "agro-ecosystem" that gives rise to it—the atmosphere, soils, fresh water, and genetic resources.

Uniting these crises as well is their origin in the decades-long process of industrialization. Industrialization rolls along according to its own peculiar logic, but it's marked by a singular focus on specialization and production to the exclusion of most of other qualities, such as health or sustainability, for example. This transformation has radically altered how we produce and distribute food, affecting the fundamental health of both humans and the planet we live on. Under industrialization, the American farm was transformed from a fairly self-sufficient entity that produced a variety of different foods into a specialized factory that produces one or maybe two widgets (corn or soybeans, chickens or hogs), reliant on the intensive use of off-farm resources (feed, oil and other energy, fertilizer, and antibiotics). Aiding this process, as I wrote recently in *Health Affairs*, has been a U.S. farm policy that for the past thirty-five years has chiefly promoted the overproduction of "cheap food." Not edible fruits and vegetables, mind you, but the overproduction of inexpensive feed-grade corn, soybeans, and a few other "commodity" crops, and the calories derived from them. Through various incentives, farmers are encouraged to produce as much as possible of these less-than-healthy foods.

"Cheap Food" Actually Costs a Lot

But this cheap food policy may no longer be affordable. As Nicholas Kristof of the *New York Times*, himself a farm boy, recently observed, "Industrial operations—essentially factories of meat and eggs—excel at manufacturing cheap food for the supermarket. But there is evidence that this model is economically viable only because it passes on health costs to the public—in the form of occasional salmonella, antibiotic-resistant diseases, polluted waters, food poisoning, and possibly certain cancers." If the long-term costs of the obesity epidemic are thrown into the mix, the "cheap food" system looks even more expensive. And health costs aside, a food system that relies so heavily on cheap, abundant fossil fuels in the form of diesel fuel, pesticides, and fertilizers may soon become unsustainable as energy costs rise.

From 1985 to 2000, the price of carbonated soft drinks, made with high fructose corn syrup, dropped 23 percent. . . . Meanwhile, the real costs of fruits and vegetables rose nearly 40 percent over the same period.

Let's use a food system perspective, where everything is related, to look at how this cheap food policy since 1974 ties to some of the health crises we've seen, starting on the farm. Predictably, we've seen a decades-long glut of corn and soybeans, and market prices for the vast majority of that time have dropped below what it actually costs farmers to produce these crops. Since the late 1990s, "emergency" payments to farmers have kept them in business despite low prices. These subsidies have now become permanent. (It's important to note that federal "cheap food" policies preceded these subsidy programs by almost twenty years. Getting rid of subsidies alone will not solve the glut of corn or soybeans.) So what's become of the excess calories stemming from this overproduction of corn and soybeans? Food processors and manufacturers have been quite creative, turning raw corn and soy into low-cost ingredients, like the added fats and sugars that factor so prominently in the snacks, sweets, beverages, and fast foods that comprise a large part of the American diet. Since 1970, the average American's consumption of corn calories—including corn flour, corn meal, hominy, and corn starch—is up 191 percent. Calories from corn sweeteners rose 359 percent over 1970 levels, to 246 calories per day. The now-ubiquitous high fructose corn syrup did not really exist in the U.S. food supply prior to 1970.

Calories consumed in the form of added fats and oils has increased 69 percent since 1970, with a 260-percent calorie increase in salad and cooking oils. Soy oil accounts for 70 percent of fats and oils eaten by Americans, and another 8 percent are corn oil. You get the picture.

In an Industrial Farm System, Production Is Everything

Retail prices for these food products have declined along with the production glut. From 1985 to 2000, the price of carbonated soft drinks, made with high fructose corn syrup, dropped 23 percent. Fats and oils, mostly from soybeans, dropped 14 percent in that time period; sugars dropped 7 percent. Meanwhile, the real costs of fruits and vegetables rose nearly 40 percent over the same period.

Change will not be simple or easy. Experts . . . are calling for public health interventions at multiple levels—local, state, national, and even international.

Still, most of the nation's corn and soybeans get fed to cattle, pigs, and poultry, either here or abroad. The federal policies that make these feed grains cheaper than a working market would allow serve as a de facto subsidy to the world's largest meat producers—one they've enjoyed for decades now. Raising animals on cheap feed grains rather than on forage or grass requires that they be centralized and, at least in the case of chickens and hogs, raised indoors. And so was born the modern-day factory farm. Tens of thousands of animals (and their manure) are crammed into one barn and then fed routine antibiotics to make them grow faster, or to keep them just healthy enough to reach slaughter despite being crammed into an indoor barn. In fact, an estimated 70 percent of all antimicrobials used in the U.S. are fed to chickens, hogs, and beef cattle for just such purposes.

All these examples illustrate the point that in an industrialized food system, production and little else matters. Not health, not antibiotic resistance, and not pollution. Given the rationale of the cheap food policy, the quantity of calories produced, and not their quality, has been of primary importance.

Intervention Is Necessary

President [Barack] Obama's cancer advisory panel recently urged the president to "use the power of your office to remove the carcinogens and other toxins from our food, water, and air that needlessly increase health care costs, cripple our nation's productivity, and devastate American lives." The [George W.] Bush-appointed panel found that "the true burden of environmentally induced cancers has been grossly underestimated." Among its recommendations: Filter your water, eat certified organic food, and avoid storing food or drink in plastics containing bisphenol A.

But putting the entire burden of responding to an unhealthy environment on individuals is wrongheaded and in the long run will prove ineffective at preventing disease. Physicians recognized this fact in becoming strong advocates for tobacco-free environments. It had become clear that without environmental change, individuals socialized to smoke and manipulated by marketing and the addictive properties of nicotine would continue to smoke. The health community also provided a critical and necessary counterweight to the financial and political might of the tobacco industry. We are at a similar point with respect to the food system. There is rising acceptance that an unhealthy food environment helps drive obesity and other chronic disease. Because that food environment is a system, change will not be simple or easy. Experts instead are calling for public health interventions at multiple levels—local, state, national, and even international.

Physicians' Voices Are Important

Many local entities are working to improve access to healthy foods at the community level, or in schools or health institutions, in part due to government stimulus funds. Because of the health implications and the respect they are afforded, physicians are critical voices for generating lasting support for these changes in their communities. . . . But the food system is national, even global in nature. To counter the decades of inertia and vested interests in an unhealthy food system, even more work will be needed. Sustained change across the country will require national leadership. Major medical associations such as the AMA [American Medical Association] and the American Academy of Pediatrics are becoming increasingly involved in food policy issues. The AMA, along with the American Dietetic Association and the American Public Health Association, has developed positions on healthy, sustainable food systems. The American Academy of Pediatrics is working with the First Lady's [Michelle Obama's] Let's Move campaign to involve physicians in writing prescriptions for parents "laying out the simple things they can do to increase healthy eating and active play."

Finally, these and other health organizations are interested in a healthier Farm Bill, the huge piece of legislation that lays the foundation not only for the food stamp program but for what farmers grow, how they grow it, and what methods they will use in the future. The Farm Bill is due to be rewritten in 2012. Individuals can join Healthy Food Action to stay apprised of this and other efforts. This national initiative provides busy health professionals with easy ways to stay informed about the links between health, food, and farm policy, and it identifies a few important policies they can weigh in on to try and make a change. Given clear science and signals that our industrialized food system is helping cause many of the health crises physicians face in their practice, the medical community can no longer afford to stand on the sidelines.

Now is the time for physicians to lead in the building of a healthier food system. A Healthy Food Bill, rather than a Farm Bill, is a good place to start.

5

Conventional Wisdom About Diet and Health Is Always Changing

Rick Berman

Rick Berman is the executive director of the Center for Consumer Freedom, a nonprofit organization that promotes personal responsibility and consumer choice.

Despite large amounts of money poured into nutrition research, expert opinion about what constitutes healthy eating is always changing. At various times, ingredients such as high fructose corn syrup and sodium have been labeled by nutrition experts as extremely damaging, but later evidence showed such claims to be exaggerated. Often, those who take up a position against a certain food or beverage have a conflict of interest that makes their opinion untrustworthy. Moderation should be the guiding principle of any diet.

In a time when seemingly every kind of food or drink has something bad associated with it, you'd think at least water would escape unscathed. But one doctor reported in the *British Medical Journal* this July [2011] that advice to drink 8 glasses of water per day is "nonsense." And drinking too much water could actually be harmful.

The lesson here isn't that water is bad or that we shouldn't drink it. Rather, it's that the so-called experts on what we eat and drink can change their minds (and often do).

In the 1970s, eggs were considered unhealthy due to their cholesterol content. Since then, scientists figured out that dietary cholesterol isn't the same thing as blood cholesterol, and the tables turned again: Eggs are now considered a health food.

Similarly, in the 1980s fat became the enemy and "low-fat" products spread like wildfire. Now that trend is starting to change as carbs are developing a stigma.

Despite how much money and expertise is poured into nutrition research, we should still be skeptical about jumping to conclusions about our food and health. Our understanding is always shifting, and it's often muddled by activists with a dog in the fight.

These days, the newest party line is that we should reduce our intake of sodium. . . . [But] recently published research discovered that salt reduction in people diagnosed with heart disease is actually associated with a more than twofold higher risk of dying.

Consider the case of high fructose corn syrup. People started to shun this corn sugar in favor of sugar from cane or beets after one hypothesis several years ago speculated that high fructose corn syrup might be especially fattening.

But once again, a nutritional about-face has occurred. Credible experts from the American Medical Association to the American Dietetic Association recognize table sugar and high fructose corn syrup are metabolized similarly by the body. And two authors of the original hypothesis later declared that sugar is sugar, whether it is made from beets, cane or corn.

These days, the newest party line is that we should reduce our intake of sodium. Sodium raises blood pressure, which in turn raises the risk of heart problems, or so the logic goes. Some "food police" activists want national salt control.

In reality, it appears that only 10 percent of the population is truly sensitive to sodium. Recently published research discovered that salt reduction in people diagnosed with heart disease is actually associated with a more than twofold higher risk of dying. Additionally, a 50 percent salt reduction was not associated with improved heart health in the general population.

And the conventional wisdom about fish consumption may soon change as well. According to a 2004 government advisory, pregnant women should eat at most two servings of fish a week due to the trace amount of mercury in seafood. Environmental and animal rights groups—concerned with preserving wild fish stocks—have latched onto this as a way to scare Americans away from eating fish.

But more than 100 experts signed an open letter last year asking the federal government to update its recommendations in light of newer research finding that the health benefits of eating fish far outweigh the hypothetical detriments. (There still hasn't been a single case of mercury poisoning in the United States from commercially bought seafood.)

A 2007 *Lancet* study found "no evidence" for concern, and further discovered that of the 9,000 pregnant women studied, those who ate the most fish had kids with the highest IQs. (Japanese children eat plenty of tuna and seem to have little trouble with math.)

What else could lie on the food horizon? It's hard to say. It may well turn out that saturated fat isn't as bad as it's made out to be.

Whatever the case, we should bet on "moderation" remaining the cornerstone of any diet. Anybody who tells you a food or ingredient is going to harm you generally has an agenda, and not your health, to promote.

6

Personal Choices Can Lead to Better Health

Anthony L. Komaroff and Robert A. Weinberg

Anthony L. Komaroff is an American physician, clinical investigator, editor, and publisher. Robert A. Weinberg is a Daniel K. Ludwig Professor for Cancer Research at MIT and an American Cancer Society Research Professor.

Studies have long proven the correlation between obesity and a sedentary lifestyle and developing heart disease and Type 2 diabetes, but now new research suggests our lifestyle choices can also play an important role in cancer. The high rates of cancer in the United States and other developed countries, compared to that in developing countries, is a strong piece of evidence for the link between lifestyle and cancer. While genes also play a role in developing cancer, lifestyle factors are something that can be changed.

New research explores the complex interactions that cause our most dreaded disease. A look into some of the steps you can take to reduce your risk.

We've known for a long time that a high-fat diet, obesity and lack of exercise can increase the risk of developing heart disease and type 2 diabetes, two conditions that affect millions of Americans. What we are finding out now is that those same lifestyle factors also play an important role in cancer. That's the bad news. The good news is that you can do something about your lifestyle. If we grew thinner, exercised regularly, avoided diets rich in red meat (substituting poultry, fish or vegetable sources of protein) and ate diets rich in fruits and vegetables, and stopped using tobacco, we would prevent 70 percent of all cancers.

[T]hose who ate a traditional Western diet had a three-fold greater likelihood of developing a recurrence of [cancer] than did those who ate a "prudent" diet rich in fruits and vegetables.

The U.S. Lifestyle and Cancer

The strongest evidence of the importance of lifestyle in cancer is that most common cancers arise at dramatically different rates in different parts of the globe. Several cancers that are extremely common in the United States—colon, prostate and breast cancer—are relatively rare in other parts of the world, occurring only 1/10th or 1/20th as often. Equally striking, when people migrate from other parts of the world to the United States, within a generation their cancer rates approach those of us whose families have lived in this country for a long time. Even if people in other parts of the world stay put, but adopt a U.S. lifestyle, their risk of cancer rises; as Japanese have embraced Western habits, their rates of colon, breast and prostate cancer have skyrocketed.

What is it about our lifestyle that raises the risk of many types of cancer? The main culprits seem to be the Western diet, obesity and physical inactivity. While we've known about the importance of tobacco and cancer for more than 50 years, we are just beginning to understand how diet, a healthy body weight and regular exercise can protect us against cancer.

A striking example of the profound influence of diet was reported last summer in *The Journal of the American Medical*

Association. Doctors determined the eating habits of patients with colon cancer in the years following surgical removal of the cancer. Over the next five years, those who ate a traditional Western diet had a threefold greater likelihood of developing a recurrence of the disease than did those who ate a "prudent" diet rich in fruits and vegetables and including only small amounts of red meat. How had diet affected these patients? The surgery clearly had not removed all their colon-cancer cells: prior to the surgery, some cells had already spread from the primary tumor. The Western diet had somehow stimulated the growth of these small deposits of residual cancer cells.

Obesity is the second most important factor in causing cancer in Western populations after tobacco, and there is evidence that maintaining a healthy weight is protective against the disease. A study by the American Cancer Society in 2003 found that the heaviest people, in comparison with the leanest, had a significantly increased risk of death from 10 different kinds of cancer in men, and from 12 different kinds in women. The most extreme examples were liver cancer in men (nearly fivefold increased risk) and uterine cancer in women (more than sixfold increased risk).

During the course of our lifetimes . . . genes are damaged in various cells throughout the body. It is these mutated genes that drive most cancers.

The Role of Exercise

Exercise has also been shown to play an important role in protecting against some cancers. For example, the Nurses' Health Study reported that women who had one or more hours per day of moderate exercise had a 30 percent lower risk of colon cancer than women who exercised less. Exercise protects against breast cancer, as well.

Lifestyle influences a person's risk for cancer by generating growth-promoting signals that affect cells primed to become cancerous, or that already are cancerous. What primes those cells to become cancerous in the first place are changes in their genes.

All tumors begin with one renegade cell. Initially the cell is just one of about 30 trillion or so in the body. It looks no different from the cells around it, and, like those cells, it divides only if the organ it's part of needs it to divide. Then, even though the organ around it has enough cells, the renegade cell begins to multiply uncontrollably: one cell becomes two, two become four, four become eight, until the descendants are beyond counting.

Cancer is ultimately a disease of malfunctioning genes. Perhaps 10 percent of all cancers occur in people who have inherited genes that make them vulnerable. In some cases, those genes are so influential the risk of cancer is very high. However, most of us are born with good genes that succeed in flawlessly organizing our growth and development. After all, our genes have been optimized by more than 600 million years of evolution; they ought to work well. During the course of our lifetimes, though, genes are damaged in various cells throughout the body. It is these mutated genes that drive most cancers.

The Molecules That Affect Gene Activity

Every cell contains growth-promoting genes called "proto-oncogenes" and growth-stopping genes called "tumor suppressor" genes. Mutations that activate a proto-oncogene can cause the gene to release an unceasing stream of growth-stimulating molecular signals that cause the cell to multiply. Conversely, mutations that inactivate tumor-suppressor genes cause their growth-stopping messages to be silenced. In most human-cancer cells, there are multiple mutations—some that activate oncogenes and some that silence tumor-suppressor genes. In other words, cancer cells have stuck accelerator pedals and faulty brakes. During our lifetime, the cells in our bodies will divide 1016 times—that's 10,000 trillion times—creating 10,000 trillion opportunities for our "start" and "stop" signals to malfunction, and for a tumor to start.

In fact, in the developed nations, only 1 to 2 percent of cancers are attributable to . . . environmental pollutants.

Another important gene, called telomerase, is turned off in healthy cells, causing the cells to die after they have doubled about 50 times. Telomerase is turned on, however, in many cancer cells, which allows them to multiply indefinitely. There are other genes that cause a cell to "commit suicide" when the cell senses that it has been damaged; if such a cell suicide gene becomes disabled, a cancer cell will be allowed to multiply.

Genes also affect a cancerous cell's ability to metastasize—to detach itself from the primary tumor, crawl through the walls of nearby small blood or lymph vessels and spread through the circulation to other parts of the body. Research published in the past year has identified sets of genes that normally are active only when cells in an embryo need to migrate from one part of the embryo to another. In cancer cells that metastasize, these long-silent genes have somehow been activated. The genes make it easy for a cell to detach itself from the tissue around it and they improve the cell's ability to move toward and through the walls of blood and lymph vessels. Recently, a small molecule called microRNA-10b was discovered to powerfully affect the ability of breast-cancer cells to metastasize. This is exciting because, at least theoretically, such small molecules are attractive targets for treatments.

But what causes the various genetic changes that lead to cancer? Mutation-inducing chemicals—mutagens—in our environment can do so. Exhibit A, of course, is tobacco smoke. However, other environmental chemicals that many people suspect of causing cancer—food preservatives, contaminants in our drinking water, pollutants pouring out of smokestacks—rarely do so. In fact, in the developed nations, only 1 to 2 percent of cancers are attributable to such environmental pollutants.

Instead, most cancer-inducing mutations occur when cells damage their own genes accidentally. Each of our cells continuously produces mutation-inducing chemicals as byproducts of its normal metabolism. When our cells generate energy by converting oxygen into water, modified oxygen molecules called "oxygen radicals" are produced. These radicals strike wildly at all the molecules in our cells, including the DNA of our genes. Although our cells have the ability to repair this damage, the protection is not perfect, and so mutations and mutant genes accumulate as we grow older.

We don't know precisely how the Western diet increases our risk of cancer. The foods we eat contain chemicals that can mutate genes and that therefore could cause cancer. For example, red meat cooked at high temperatures generates potent mutagens called heterocyclic amines. Foods contain many different chemicals, and those chemicals are transformed in our body into many other chemicals, making it very difficult to pinpoint just what it is about the Western diet that raises our risk of cancer. But there is no doubt that it does.

Obesity and Cancer

While we don't really understand yet why obesity fosters cancer, cancer promoters could play a role. Obesity leads to high levels of insulin-like growth factor (IGF-1) in the circulation: theoretically, this could protect early-stage cancer cells scattered throughout the body from dying, since insulin-like growth factor inhibits the action of cell suicide genes. Inflammation also may explain the link between obesity and cancer. Inflammation is a normal body process designed to rid a tissue of infection and to heal it following injury. Cells of the immune system orchestrate inflammation, and some of the weapons they deploy are chemical signals called cytokines. Often, inflammation is brief. If your skin is cut, or develops a bacterial infection, inflammation aids in repairing the wound or eliminating the bacteria. Having done its job, inflammation then subsides.

Our growing understanding of cancer genes, and how they are influenced by cancer-promoting chemical signals, already has led to important new diagnostic tests and powerful new treatments.

However, if you have a condition that inflammation cannot rapidly heal, then the inflammation becomes protracted, chronic. The injured tissue is constantly bathed in growth-promoting cytokines that tell stem cells in the tissue to begin multiplying, in order to replace the cells that have been injured and destroyed. If any of these stem cells already have acquired mutations that make them precancerous, cytokines that encourage those cells to multiply can increase the risk that a tumor will start. For example, stomach tissue that can turn cancerous when it is chronically inflamed in response to the bacteria that cause many stomach ulcers. The same thing happens to the lining of gallbladders after years of irritation from gallstones, or to the liver after years of infection with hepatitis viruses.

What does inflammation have to do with obesity? Fat cells release inflammatory chemicals into the circulation that can stimulate the growth of cancer cells. The more overweight we are, the greater the level of inflammatory signals. It is possible that these cytokines act as cancer promoters, but much more research is needed to determine whether that is true.

Regular moderate exercise lowers the levels of both IGF-1 and cytokines in our blood, and it does so even if the exercise does not lead to a healthy weight. It is possible that the lowered levels of these cancer promoters are one explanation for the protective effect of regular exercise. Blood-estrogen levels are lowered by regular exercise in women, and this may be another way that regular exercise protects against getting breast cancer.

Our growing understanding of cancer genes, and how they are influenced by cancer-promoting chemical signals, already has led to important new diagnostic tests and powerful new treatments, and will likely lead to even more important advances in the future. But epidemiological studies of lifestyle and cancer have given us the power, today, to reduce our risk of cancer. While it isn't easy to make changes in lifestyle, it can happen. There are many fewer people using tobacco in the United States today than two generations ago, when the risks of tobacco were first revealed. It may take another two generations to further reduce tobacco use, and to improve our diets, weight and exercise patterns, but it can happen. If it does, our grandchildren are likely to look back at our generation, scratch their heads and wonder why it took so long for us to escape the disease that many of us feared the most, by simple changes in the way we led our lives.

7

Residents of "Food Deserts" Lack Access to Nutritious Foods

Michele Ver Ploeg

Michele Ver Ploeg is an economist on the staff of the Economic Research Service (ERS), a division of the US Department of Agriculture that provides economic information and research.

A poor diet can lead to obesity and diabetes. The US Department of Agriculture has mapped the locations of supermarkets and large grocery stores throughout the country in order to determine those areas that may lack access to nutritious and affordable food. Low-income neighborhoods that are located more than a mile from a supermarket have been designated "food deserts." Using these and other criteria, the Department of Agriculture estimates that 11.5 million people, or 4.1 percent of the US population, lack access to affordable and nutritious food.

Some neighborhoods in the United States, particularly those in low-income areas, have been dubbed "food deserts" because residents do not live near supermarkets or other food retailers that carry affordable and nutritious food. Low-income residents of these neighborhoods and those who lack transportation rely more on smaller neighborhood stores that may not carry healthy foods or may offer them only at higher prices.

Michele Ver Ploeg, "Access to Affordable, Nutritious Food Is Limited in 'Food Deserts,'" *Amber Waves*, USDA, March, 2010.

A lack of healthy options could lead to poor diets and to diet-related conditions such as obesity or diabetes. If low-income households in food deserts can only purchase food at higher prices, they may be more prone to food insecurity—not having enough food for active, healthy living.

Supermarket Access Is a Problem for Some

Defining what lack of access to affordable and nutritious food means and estimating how many people are affected by living in food deserts is not straightforward. A number of different measures are possible. ERS [Economic Research Service] began its investigation into access by mapping the availability of affordable and nutritious food across the country. Because it is too costly to survey the types of foods and prices offered in every store, ERS used the availability of supermarkets and large grocery stores (including discount and supercenter stores) as a proxy for the availability of affordable, nutritious food.

11.5 million people, or 4.1 percent of the U.S. population, have low incomes and live in low-income neighborhoods that are more than a mile from a supermarket.

A 2006 directory of supermarkets and large grocery stores throughout the continental U.S. was used to examine distance to the nearest supermarket or large grocery store. Researchers focused on populations that may be particularly vulnerable to access problems—those in low-income families and low-income neighborhoods, as well as households without access to a personal vehicle.

According to data from the latest census (2000), about 23.5 million people, or 8.4 percent of the U.S. population, live in low-income neighborhoods that are more than a mile from a supermarket. Low-income neighborhoods are areas where more than 40 percent of the population has income less than or equal to 200 percent of the Federal poverty threshold ($44,000 per year for a family of four in 2008).

While all the people living in these neighborhoods are affected by their neighborhoods' characteristics, not all of those living in low-income neighborhoods are poor. Better-off residents in low-income areas are likely to have personal vehicles to get to supermarkets outside their immediate neighborhoods or sufficient financial resources to use food-delivery services. Just over half of all people in low-income neighborhoods have incomes that are below 200 percent of the Federal poverty level. Thus, 11.5 million people, or 4.1 percent of the U.S. population, have low incomes and live in low-income neighborhoods that are more than a mile from a supermarket. . . .

Some neighborhoods lacking supermarkets may be served by smaller grocery or convenience stores which may offer some healthy foods, but often at higher prices than supermarkets.

Lack of Transportation Creates a Barrier

Perhaps the best measure of whether someone who lives far from a grocery store faces obstacles to accessing affordable and nutritious food is whether or not he or she has a car. Access to a car allows people to leave the food desert and shop at supermarkets and large grocery stores outside of their neighborhoods. But not everyone has regular access to a car. About 2.3 million, or 2.2 percent, of households in the continental U.S. live more than a mile from a supermarket and do not have access to a vehicle. For these households, lack of transportation poses a likely barrier to accessing affordable and nutritious food.

The 2.2 percent of households and 4.1 percent of individuals who face food access barriers are in line with the 2001

Food Security Supplement of the U.S. Census Bureau's Current Population Survey, which asked respondents whether they had enough food and the kinds of foods they wanted. Those who responded that they did not have enough food or the kinds of foods they wanted were asked why and whether access-related factors, such as the availability of desired foods or difficulty in getting to a store, were the causes. Responses to these direct questions show that nearly 6 percent of all U.S. households faced access-related problems in obtaining food.

Low-Income Consumers Shop Outside Food Deserts When They Can

Some neighborhoods lacking supermarkets may be served by smaller grocery or convenience stores which may offer some healthy foods, but often at higher prices than supermarkets. Higher prices at these food retailers compound the problem of limited access to healthy foods. Residents unable to get to larger stores outside of their neighborhood are more likely to be food insecure if they cannot afford to buy all the food they need. In addition, higher prices for groceries in these neighborhoods may make local fast food or carryout foods relatively more affordable.

To understand better the prices paid by low-income consumers, a 2009 study by an ERS researcher and colleagues used household-level purchase data to analyze differences in prices paid for the same food items by consumers with different levels of income. The data covered the food purchases of approximately 40,000 representative U.S. households.

The analysis shows that many low-income consumers can find lower prices, but consumers with very low incomes may not be able to get to stores that offer these low prices. Consumers with annual incomes between $8,000 and $30,000 paid the least of all income groups for the same food items. More worrisome, however, is the finding that households with annual incomes less than $8,000 paid slightly more—between

0.5 to 1.3 percent—for the same foods than those with incomes between $8,000 and $30,000. Households with incomes
over $100,000 per year paid the most for the same food
items—between 2 to 3 percent more than poorer households.

---

*A food-desert neighborhood may lack a supermarket or
large grocery store because of the costs food retailers face
when building and/or operating a store in those locations.*

ERS also analyzed the prices consumers paid at four different store formats (grocery, convenience, discount/
supercenters, and "other") for three frequently purchased
foods—milk, ready-to-eat cereal, and bread. Characteristics of
the foods, such as fat content of milk or product size, were
controlled. The results show that convenience store prices
were higher than prices at grocery stores—milk prices were 5
percent higher; cereal, 25 percent; and bread, 10 percent.

However, food purchases at convenience stores make up
just 2 to 3 percent of total food expenditures for low-income
consumers. Low- and middle-income consumers are more
likely than higher income households to purchase food at supercenters, where prices are lower.

Research sponsored by USDA's [US Department of Agri-
culture] Food and Nutrition Service (FNS) in the mid-1990s
on the food-shopping behavior of participants in the Food
Stamp Program (now known as the Supplemental Nutrition
Assistance Program, or SNAP) corroborates these findings.
Close to 90 percent of all food stamp benefits were redeemed
at supermarkets or large grocery stores—a percentage that, according to more recent FNS data, has not changed much. Further, while food stamp participants, on average, lived 1.8 miles
from the nearest supermarket, they traveled an average of 4.9
miles to get to the store they most often used to buy groceries.

Some Neighborhoods Are More Attractive for Supermarkets

A food-desert neighborhood may lack a supermarket or large grocery store because of the costs food retailers face when building and/or operating a store in those locations. The price of land or rent may be higher in food-desert neighborhoods. Zoning rules, such as the amount of parking required for new businesses, could make it more costly to develop a new store. Small grocery stores or convenience stores may face lower rent and parking costs, but they may have a harder time accommodating equipment or space needed for fresh produce or perishable products. Some food deserts may be far from convenient delivery routes, while others may have crime and security concerns that increase a store's operating costs.

Efforts to provide nutritional guidance or to change dietary habits will be ineffective if it is too difficult or expensive for people to get to stores that carry healthier foods.

Consumers' demographic and economic characteristics, buying habits, and tastes also may explain why stores do not locate in some areas or carry particular foods. More densely populated neighborhoods and those with increasing populations are often able to support more stores. As a result, some less densely populated rural areas, or urban areas with diminishing populations, may have fewer supermarkets. Food expenditures increase as income rises, which may explain why higher income neighborhoods have more supermarkets than some lower income neighborhoods.

One trend in supermarket development has been increasingly larger stores, such as supercenters. This store model relies on substantial parcels of land for the store and adequate parking, as well as roadways to accommodate large delivery trucks and customer access. Supercenters and other very large stores may not be as feasible in dense urban environments or in small rural towns that lack sufficient transportation infrastructure.

Some supermarket chains have developed smaller store formats that fit into denser urban environments, such as the Fresh and Easy Neighborhood Markets, a subsidiary of Tesco. These stores have opened in California and parts of the Southwest. Other supermarket chains have developed store formats designed specifically to serve low-income and bargain shoppers. These "hard discount" grocery stores, such as ALDI or Food4Less, are often smaller than the average supermarket and carry fewer products—sometimes selling only store brands or offering a limited range of product sizes.

Improving Access and Encouraging Healthy Choices

Policies to encourage the supply of affordable and nutritious food in underserved areas, such as zoning modifications and grants or loans for new store development, will not affect residents' health if they do not change their food-purchasing behavior or do not have the time or knowledge to prepare healthier foods. At the same time, efforts to provide nutritional guidance or to change dietary habits will be ineffective if it is too difficult or expensive for people to get to stores that carry healthier foods.

Some public policy interventions to increase access to affordable and nutritious food simultaneously promote healthier choices among residents and a better supply of those choices. For example, New York City has implemented the Healthy Bodegas and Health Bucks programs to address disparities in access to some specific healthy foods. The Healthy Bodega Initiative recruits bodegas or small corner stores in nutritionally vulnerable areas to increase their offerings of low-fat milk, fruit, and vegetables. The city provides promotional and educational materials to entice people to purchase the new offerings and to encourage bodegas to participate.

The Health Bucks program, which began in 2005, offers $2 coupons to people in vulnerable areas for the purchase of fresh fruit and vegetables at participating farmers' markets, generating business for farmers and reducing food access barriers for residents. The program also gives SNAP participants an additional $2 in Health Bucks for every $5 in SNAP benefits they spend at participating farmers' markets.

8

In Depth Briefing:
America's "Food Deserts"

The Week

The Week *is an international news and media digest.*

The US Department of Agriculture defines a food desert as a census district where at least 20 percent of individuals are below the poverty line and 33 percent live over a mile from the nearest supermarket; living in a food desert is thought to be a risk factor that is contributing to America's obesity and diabetes epidemics. However, the real cause of obesity is not lack of access to supermarkets, it is excessive access to fast-food restaurants. There are now five fast-food restaurants for every supermarket in the United States, and some studies show that consuming large quantities of fast food results in symptoms that mimic drug addiction.

What is a 'food desert'?

A community in which residents must travel at least a mile to buy fresh meat, dairy products, and vegetables. More precisely, the U.S. Department of Agriculture (USDA) defines a food desert as any census district where at least 20 percent of the inhabitants are below the poverty line and 33 percent live over a mile from the nearest supermarket (or in rural areas, more than 10 miles). Approximately 23.5 million Americans live in a food desert, says the USDA, including vast, rural swaths of West Virginia, Ohio, and Kentucky, as well as urban areas like

Detroit, Chicago, and New York City. The government believes food deserts are contributing to the obesity epidemic in the U.S., by forcing the rural and urban poor to rely on processed foods and fast food, instead of fresh meat, vegetables, and fruit. Today, more than one third of adult Americans are obese.

The real problem ... is the existence of "food swamps," filled with convenience stores selling calorie-loaded packaged foods, gallon cups of soda, and other sugar-loaded beverages, and fast-food chains peddling burgers.

Can this trend be reversed?

The government thinks it can, if major supermarkets open stores in blighted areas and stock affordable healthy food options. First Lady Michelle Obama's "Let's Move!" campaign, which aims to reduce childhood obesity, has taken a lead role in this effort, and recently scored a major coup by convincing Walmart, SuperValu, and Walgreens to open or expand 1,500 grocery stores in food deserts. The involvement of large retail firms has "the potential to be a game-changer for kids and communities all across this country," Obama said. "More parents will have a fresh food retailer right in their community, so they can feed their families the way they want." But not everyone shares the First Lady's optimism; in fact, some critics say opening new stores and markets in so-called food deserts will have little or no impact on how people eat.

Why would that be?

First of all, the critics say, the very concept of a food desert may be a mirage. One recent University of Washington study found that only 15 percent of people shop for groceries within their own census areas; most of us, in other words, are accustomed to traveling a few miles to stock our pantries. Critics also point out that the USDA takes only supermarkets into account when deciding whether an area is a food desert. Smaller grocery stores, farmers markets, and roadside stalls aren't included. Moreover, the vast majority of households (93 percent) in food deserts have access to a car, and can easily drive to grocery stores over a mile from their homes.

So what's the real problem?

Many people simply like fast food better. A recent University of North Carolina (UNC) study of the eating habits of 5,000 people over 15 years found that living near a supermarket had little impact on whether people had healthy diets. But living close to fast-food outlets did. The real problem, the study found, is the existence of "food swamps," filled with convenience stores selling calorie-loaded packaged foods, gallon cups of soda, and other sugar-loaded beverages, and fast-food chains peddling burgers, fries, and fried chicken on almost every street corner. That's no exaggeration: There are now five fast-food restaurants for every supermarket in the U.S.

Studies have repeatedly found that the consequences of bingeing on high-calorie, high-fat foods mimic the effects of drug addiction.

Why do people choose the 'bad' food?

Fast food is generally cheaper, and doesn't need to be prepared and cooked, so it's more convenient. Studies have also shown that the huge jolt of fat, salt, and sugar fast food delivers can be almost as addictive as hard drugs (see below). Then there's the advertising factor: Fast-food companies spend about $4.2 billion a year marketing their products as life's ultimate rewards, through saliva-producing ads depicting cheese-and-pepperoni-covered pizzas, juicy double cheeseburgers, and steaming French fries.

Can these preferences be changed?

The UNC study suggests using zoning laws to restrict the number of fast-food restaurants in low-income neighborhoods. Los Angeles has already experimented with this approach, having imposed a one-year moratorium on the building of fast-food restaurants over a 32-square-mile area. City officials say the results were successful, and have now imposed permanent zoning restrictions on fast-food chains in the poorer, southern part of the city. "We have already attracted new sit-down restaurants, full-service grocery stores, and healthy food alternatives," said City Councilwoman Jan Perry. "Ultimately, this action is about providing choices."

Will people choose healthy food?

Not necessarily. Many Americans have little experience eating or preparing broccoli, asparagus, and other produce; in fact, only 26 percent of the nation's adults now eat three servings of vegetables a day. The poor, in particular, have become so accustomed to salty packaged foods and sugary beverages that they find fresh food bland, strange, and off-putting. "It's simplistic thinking that if you put fruits and vegetables there, they'll buy it," said Barry Popkin, author of the UNC study. "You have to encourage it, you need advertising, you need support." Changing Americans' diets, in other words, won't be as simple as telling them to eat their peas.

Fast-food junkies

If it sometimes seems that Americans are addicted to fast food, it might be that we actually are. Studies have repeatedly found that the consequences of bingeing on high-calorie, high-fat foods mimic the effects of drug addiction. A recent study by the Scripps Research Institute found that gorging on fast food actually changes the brain's chemical makeup, making it more difficult to trigger the release of dopamine (aka "the pleasure chemical"). That means fast-food addicts need to eat more and more to feel happy—the same way users of cocaine and other drugs, for example, need to keep upping their dosages to get high. An earlier study, by Princeton University, found that rats who were fed and then withdrawn from a high-fat, high-sugar diet exhibited similar symptoms—chattering teeth and the shakes—to junkies going cold turkey. "Drugs give a bigger effect," said study author Bart Hoebel, "but it's essentially the same process."

9

Federal Guidelines for Food and Health Are Often Confusing

Jane Black

Jane Black is a staff writer for The Washington Post.

The US Department of Agriculture (USDA) regularly updates dietary guidelines for Americans. The guidelines affect many aspects of life, including school breakfast and lunch programs, SNAP (the USDA's Supplemental Nutrition Assistance Program, formerly food stamps), and information provided on food packaging. Critics claim that the process of arriving at guidelines is so vulnerable to political pressure from the food industry that the advice the government provides is not trustworthy.

Every five years the federal government updates its dietary guidelines for Americans. This year [2010], with most Americans overweight or obese and at risk of high blood pressure, policymakers are working to reinvent the familiar food pyramid and develop advice that is simple and blunt enough to help turn the tide.

Dietary Guidelines Make an Impact

Although most people do not read them, the guidelines have broad impact on Americans' lives. They dictate what is served in school breakfast and lunch, in education materials used by

SNAP [the USDA's Supplemental Nutrition Assistance Program]—formerly called food stamps—and in the development of information on the nutrition labels of food packages. They also underpin education materials that are available in community centers, doctors' offices and hospitals.

What the guidelines will say when they are unveiled in December [2010] is still under wraps. But the interagency committee is searching for new ways to communicate lessons about healthful eating and is working to make the food pyramid "more meaningful and engaging," said Dr. Robert Post, deputy director of the U.S. Department of Agriculture's Center for Nutrition and Policy Promotion that is leading the development of the guidelines.

Healthy eating has gained a high profile through Michelle Obama's "Let's Move" initiative to fight childhood obesity. But historically, the government has shied away from offering controversial advice. And with food, everything is controversial: A boost for one type of food in the guidelines can be viewed as a threat by providers of competing products. The result, critics say, is a nutritional education system so politically influenced that it is ineffective.

According to a study conducted by the International Food Information Council, an industry trade group, 46 percent of consumers agree that food and health information is often confusing and conflicting.

Politics Play a Role

This year's process appears to be no exception. In public comments, the meat lobby has opposed strict warnings on sodium that could cast a negative light on lunch meats. The milk lobby has expressed concerns about warnings to cut back on added sugars, lest chocolate- and strawberry-flavored milks fall from favor. Several members of the Massachusetts congressional delegation also weighed in against added-sugar restrictions in defense of the cranberry.

"This is the real test of whether this administration is serious about helping people to change their diets," said Margo Wootan, director of nutrition at the Washington-based public health watchdog Center for Science in the Public Interest.

Even if the political will is there, developing useful advice remains a challenge. It has to be broad enough to apply to myriad ethnic and other taste preferences. It must be prescriptive enough to provide guidance to shoppers who have to choose between tens of thousands of products on grocery store shelves and are befuddled by ever-changing nutrition information.

Health Information Should Be Clear and Simple

According to a study conducted by the International Food Information Council, an industry trade group, 46 percent of consumers agree that food and health information is often confusing and conflicting. And no wonder: Eggs, once shunned because of cholesterol, are now praised for their protein content. Carbohydrates, once exiled from fashionable plates, are back in vogue, provided they come from whole grains. This year, 88 percent of Americans were unable to accurately estimate the number of calories they should consume, up from 85 percent in 2009.

By avoiding blunt messages about what not to eat, the government has spoken in a way that baffles consumers.

"We can't load people down with different messages," said the USDA's Post. "We have to focus on practical, simple, easily applied messages that show action that consumers can take."

The food industry has lobbied hard to ensure that the government emphasizes carrots, not sticks, in nutrition messages. Consumers want control over their diet, lobbyists say, and they resent messages that dictate what should and should not be eaten.

Policymakers have long seen the wisdom of this strategy. And when they have strayed from it, the political heat has been intense. In 1977, a Senate select committee led by Sen. George McGovern (D-S.D.) was forced to beat a hasty retreat after it initially recommended that Americans could cut their intake of saturated fat by reducing their consumption of red meat and dairy products. Its revised guidelines suggested choosing "meat, poultry and fish that will reduce saturated-fat intake."

Guidelines Rarely Recommend Eating Less

McGovern, whose constituents included many cattle ranchers, lost his seat in 1980. Since then, in case after case, the guidelines have refrained from suggesting that Americans eat less of just about anything.

Public health advocates say that kind of vacuum is precisely the problem: By avoiding blunt messages about what not to eat, the government has spoken in a way that baffles consumers.

Translating scientific data into clear and useful recommendations poses political pitfalls.

"The only time they talk about food is if it's an 'eat more' message," said Marion Nestle, a professor of nutrition at New York University and a longtime critic of the food industry. "If it's a question of eating less, then they talk about nutrients."

Moreover, decades of positive advice to eat more vegetables clearly has not persuaded Americans to do so. In September, the Centers for Disease Control and Prevention released a nationwide study showing only 26 percent of adults eat vegetables three or more times a day—far short of national targets.

For the Obama administration, the dietary guidelines offer an opportunity—one that does not require a vote in Congress. (The anti-hunger lobby and rebellious Democrats recently stalled passage of a child nutrition bill that was a centerpiece of the first lady's Let's Move initiative.)

Science and Politics Are in Conflict

But as in the past, translating scientific data into clear and useful recommendations poses political pitfalls. The advisory committee's emphasis on a "plant-based" diet, for example, has caused much consternation among the powerful egg and meat lobbies who say the term might be misunderstood as advocating a vegetarian diet. (In fact, plant-based is defined as a diet that emphasizes fruits and vegetables but includes moderate amounts of meat, eggs and milk.) The Salt Institute has mounted an aggressive campaign to battle the recommended 35 percent reduction in the recommended allowance for sodium, saying the advice amounted to an "uncontrolled trial on more than 300 million Americans" that could result in greater obesity as individuals eat more to satisfy their sodium appetite.

By law, the guidelines must reflect the recommendations from the scientific advisory committee. But policymakers have broad discretion about how and whether to update the food pyramid.

The Food Pyramid Has Been Deemed a Failure

The current version, called MyPyramid, was unveiled in 2005 and has been widely judged a failure. Where the original pyramid placed staples in the broad bottom of the triangle and special-occasion foods at the narrow top, MyPyramid is abstract. Six swaths of color, representing grains, vegetables, fruits, oils, milk, and meat and beans, sweep from the apex of the triangle to base. The width of the color bands, which is often difficult to distinguish, is meant to represent the amount of each food group people should eat. For details about serving sizes and other information, consumers must access the Web site, MyPyramid.gov.

"We've heard a lot of views about the pyramid," said Post. "The questions we're asking are: Does it convey everything we want? Does it convey anything meaningful?"

Post gave no details about what new concepts the agency is considering. But sources say the CDC, an adviser to the process, has requested information on a proposal that would replace the pyramid with a plate of food that visually demonstrates a healthful meal—an approach developed by the National Cancer Institute.

Whatever policymakers decide, the guidelines must take a new approach, said Linda Van Horn, a professor of preventive medicine at Northwestern University and chairman of the 2010 dietary guidelines advisory committee: "What has been done till now isn't working. To do nothing more effective than we have means that five years from now we'll be in an even worse situation. And that would be unconscionable."

10

Doctors Should Stress Food Variety, Minimal Processing, and Moderation

Marion Nestle

Marion Nestle is a professor in the department of Nutrition, Food Studies, and Public Health at New York University.

Nutrition is important to health, and doctors should be prepared to provide advice about diet on a routine basis. However, today's health-care environment limits the amount of time available for talking with patients about nutrition. By focusing on a few key points, physicians can cover most of what patients need to know about diet in a small amount of time.

What should doctors tell patients about nutrition? It intrigues me how often I've been asked this question since the late 1970s, when I first was involved in developing a nutrition education program for students and practitioners in the medical and other health professions at the UCSF [University of California, San Francisco] School of Medicine.

Then, as now, it was evident that nearly every patient who landed at San Francisco General Hospital, or even the university's teaching hospital, would benefit from some kind of nutrition intervention. At a minimum, it would have helped to make sure they were fed on a regular basis.

Everyone Wants Advice About Food

It was equally obvious that almost everyone who visited the outpatient clinics either asked for or needed advice about their dietary habits.

Then, as now, few medical students were taught much about basic principles of nutrition, let alone the details of what they needed to know to help patients manage their illness or address less acute dietary concerns.

But I am a realist. In today's health care environment, even doctors with advanced nutrition training don't have time to use it. I blame this on how our health care system systematically rewards health professionals for treating disease but does little to promote health and prevent disease.

How doctors need to advise patients about nutrition depends on whom they are talking to. If they're dealing with patients who are sick or in hospitals, doctors need to discuss how dietary changes and improvements will help patients recover from their illness and prevent further disease.

It takes only a minute to explain that healthy eating simply means attending to food variety, minimal processing, and moderation.

But the task here really refers to what to say to healthy patients who want to stay that way. In the outpatient setting, what doctors do and say is profoundly important. Doctors are authority figures, and there is no question that patients take their advice seriously even if they don't always follow it.

In my experience as a patient, primary care doctors routinely ask us about drugs, cigarettes, and alcohol, but hardly ever about what foods we eat.

Even if there is only a minute during which to address these issues, diet should be added to the list. Asking about diet can produce great benefits. If nothing else, the mere asking of the question conveys the idea that the doctor cares what the patient eats and wants the patient to understand that diet matters to health.

Not a Lot of Time to Talk About Nutrition

But, again, I am a realist. I am well aware of the fact of time constraints, and my list of suggestions for what doctors should tell patients about diet and health is necessarily short. Fortunately, it doesn't take long to tell patients that what they eat matters to their health. It takes only a minute to explain that healthy eating simply means attending to food variety, minimal processing, and moderation.

Variety means selecting many different kinds of foods from the various food groups: meat, dairy, fruits, vegetables, grains. Variety is a fundamental principle of nutrition because foods vary in nutrient content. Choosing different kinds of foods within and among food groups compensates for differences in nutrient content without anyone having to think about them. People who consume adequate amounts of varied diets rarely exhibit nutrient deficiencies (vitamin D, actually a hormone, may be the one exception). Diets that restrict one or another food group are the kinds most likely to be deficient in one or another nutrient.

Patients need to hear from doctors about the importance of maintaining a healthy weight through balancing food intake with physical activity.

Minimal processing means that the foods should be as close as possible to how they came from the animal or plant. The more thoroughly a food is processed, the less it resembles its plant or animal origins. Processing removes nutrients from foods (even if some vitamins and minerals are added back) and typically adds salt, sugar, and calories to disguise these effects.

Minimal processing excludes foods high in salt and sugars and low in fiber. It also excludes sugary sodas and juice drinks. These are popularly known as "junk foods" or "foods of minimal nutritional value." They are best consumed rarely and in small amounts.

My additional rules about minimal processing are only slightly facetious: Don't eat anything with more than five ingredients. Don't eat anything with an ingredient you can't pronounce.

Moderation is about balancing calorie intake with expenditure and maintaining a healthy weight through food choices and physical activity. Today, overweight and obesity are leading risk factors for chronic disease and disability. Patients need to hear from doctors about the importance of maintaining a healthy weight through balancing food intake with physical activity.

Patients expect their doctors to care about what they eat, to ask about their dietary practices, and to answer questions about food issues they have heard or read about.

Nutrition Advice Should Be Personalized

These are general principles. Beyond them, nutrition advice must be personalized to the particular individual or family. To do that quickly:

- Ask patients what they and their children eat. You can start with a waiting room questionnaire that probes typical intake of foods and supplements. This alone will make it clear that you think diet is worth discussing.

- Screen the responses for variety, minimal processing, moderation, and excessive or unusual supplement use. Note whether body weights are within healthy ranges.

Ask someone on your staff to do the screening and mark items that could use attention.

- Reassure patients whose diets are varied, minimally balanced, and moderate that they are doing wonderful things for their health and should keep doing what they are doing.

- Refer observations that need further discussion to a nutritionist.

This last point means that doctors don't have to do it all. Making it clear to patients that diet matters is often enough to encourage them to make better dietary choices. Patients who seem unlikely to respond or who need further discussion and intervention can be referred to a well-trained nutritionist who is skilled at dealing with such issues.

These days, the effects of food on health are matters of great public interest and concern. Patients expect their doctors to care about what they eat, to ask about their dietary practices, and to answer questions about food issues they have heard or read about. A referral can help with the questions, but any doctor ought to be able to care and ask—and do much public good as a result.

11

A Plant-Based Diet Is Healthier than the Standard Western Diet

Malavika Velayanikal

Malavika Velayanikal is an author for DNA (Daily News & Analysis).

More and more people are converting to vegetarianism or vegan-ism because of the treatment of animals by the meat industry. However, the benefits of vegetarian and vegan diets extend be-yond animal welfare. Veganism, a diet which excludes any kind of animal product, such as meat, milk, and eggs, promotes a healthy body more than a traditional Western diet. Most lifestyle diseases, such as cancer, obesity, and diabetes, can be prevented by the right diet. A plant-based diet is the best choice to main-tain health.

They don't seem uncanny. They could well fall under the 'normal' tag. Yet, fundamentally, there's much extraordi-nary about them. They are vegans. They take compassion all the way—in principle and action, abstain from the use of any product or habit or behaviour that might, at any stage of its development, have involved harm upon any sentient creature. Veganism (pronounced vee-gun-ism) goes beyond a diet which excludes any kind of animal products, such as meat, fish, milk and milk products, eggs, honey, animal fat or gelatin. It is a lifestyle of compassion, vegans in the city say.

Bangalore has a burgeoning clan of committed vegans, who vouch for the lifestyle citing not just a clear conscience, but also a healthy body.

Most lifestyle diseases, diabetes, cancer, and other auto-immune disorders can be prevented by the right diet.

Making the Choice to Become a Vegan

Dilip Bafna, the founder of the Vegan Bengaluru Club, says he wasn't aware of veganism when he adopted it 17 years ago. He was always involved with animal welfare activities and was a vegetarian. "Somewhere along, I felt 'welfare' wasn't enough. There's more to do. Animal rights are equally important. In 1993, I shunned milk products and all kinds of animal products. It was only two years later that I realised that I am called a 'vegan,'" he laughs. There were only about 15 vegans in India then, he says. Dilip Bafna started an NGO, Animal Rights Fund, in 1999, and began to network among the like-minded. Slowly, he discovered more vegans—272 precisely—and decided to start a club. He got in touch with all of them, and called for a meeting. "Only one person came in—Ravi. But we started the club," Bafna says. Not yet two years since inception, the Vegan Bengaluru Club has 66 members now.

A member of the club, Isabel Putinja turned vegan two years ago. She is a Canadian who moved to Bangalore a few years ago and is an Odissi dancer besides a writer. Like most other vegans, Putinja has always been fiercely compassionate towards animals. "The Disney movies I used to watch as a child perhaps had something to do with it," she says. She became a vegetarian when a teenager. "My parents thought it would only be a phase, but I stuck to it."

It was a homeopathic workshop by Dr Nandita Shah in Auroville that prodded Putinja to veganism. "The doctor demonstrated how a vegan diet is the best for health. Most lifestyle diseases, diabetes, cancer, and other auto-immune disorders can be prevented by the right diet. I decided to try it for a month." She started using soy milk, and began using substitutes like vegan cheese and tofu for dairy products. She found it to be tasty and switching to veganism wasn't half as tough as she had imagined it to be. She discovered a whole new vegan menu, which salved her conscience while not compromising on taste. Her husband, who she says eats meat outside home, loves her vegan dishes as well. "It's so much easier in India to be a vegan unlike in most European countries like France and Belgium. Here, vegetarianism is common and going vegan is like an extension of that," she says.

To Manuj Chandra, veganism is the only right way to live. . . . He finds slaughter of fauna unpardonable.

Sandesh Raju became a vegan eight years ago. His family is traditionally into silk production, and he remembers asking his father as a child: "How many silkworms did we kill for this sari?" The figure always ran in millions, and he used to feel a stab. Years later, an animal rights activist, Poornima Harish, and Maneka Gandhi through her emphatic videos convinced Raju to go vegan. And that wasn't it. He managed to convince his father to give up the silk business and his mother became a vegetarian!

Veganism Is Compassionate and Improves Health

For Prasad Hariharan, veganism happened due to health reasons. "Milk products were an important part of my daily diet. I often used to have stomach upsets and would catch cold frequently too. A friend suggested that stopping dairy products will help. And it so did," Hariharan says. Giving up milk tea, he says, was the toughest hurdle. "But now, I have found so many different types of vegan milk that I can have a tea with a different milk every day of the week," he says. He says vegan diet also improved his stamina in a big way. He is an avid cyclist. "I can safely say that I have 20 times more stamina now. Recently, I cycled 180 km to Bheemeshwari and back without getting exhausted." Isabel Putinja says veganism built her endurance levels too. She cites the example of ten-time Olympic medalist Carl Lewis, who switched to veganism to up his stamina.

"Being vegan requires you to be diligent. Anything we pick up from the shelves, we read the fine print. 'Milk solids' is the term to watch out for," says Putinja. You have to be careful about cosmetics as well. Doesn't it drastically reduce choice? Not really, she says. Parle has a whole range of vegan biscuits and other products. There are so many herbal cosmetics available. And shoes, she says pointing at the handsome pair on her feet, Bata has a whole range of leather-look-alikes. If you have the conviction to be truly compassionate, these are just tiny bits of tweaking you need to do, she says.

To Manuj Chandra, veganism is the only right way to live. The rationalist in him is outraged by the meat industry. He finds slaughter of fauna unpardonable. The flora that goes into feeding the livestock is also pointless, he feels. "You have to feed an animal 12 kg of foodgrains for half-a-kilo meat. Precious rainforest are being cut down to grow grains to feed the meat industry. The actual cost of one hamburger is $200, and we get it for less than $2. It's an intricate web of suicide," Chandra says. He says the high rate of osteoporosis and breast cancer in the country is directly linked to India being the biggest producer as well as consumer of milk and its by-products. Veganism to him was inevitable. "I don't know of any better way an individual can make so much difference to conserving the flora and fauna," he says.

You can't really draw a line when it comes to compassion, can you?

12

A High-Protein, Low-Carb Diet Is Healthier than the Standard Western Diet

Conner Middelmann-Whitney

Conner Middelmann-Whitney is a nutritionist and health writer. She is the author of Zest for Life: The Mediterranean Anti-Cancer Diet.

Research shows that a low-carbohydrate, protein-rich diet may be healthier than the industrialized Western diet. Many cancers seem to be associated with high blood glucose levels, and it appears that restricting glucose in the diet reduces the risk of cancer.

Hitherto known mostly as a weight-loss method, low-carb eating may also protect us against cancer. A new study highlights how heavy intakes of sugar and refined carbohydrates typical of the industrialised Western diet could be a factor fueling the worldwide cancer epidemic.

The study, published next month [July 2011] in *Cancer Research*, indicates that eating a low-carbohydrate, high-protein diet may reduce the risk of cancer and slow the growth of tumors already present.

Glucose Fuels Growth of Cancer Cells

Although the study was conducted in mice, its authors said the findings are relevant to humans: "The fact that human blood glucose can be significantly reduced with low-carbohydrate diets, and the association of many cancers with high blood glucose levels, suggest that our findings are very relevant to human cancers, particularly cancers that have been associated with higher blood glucose and/or insulin levels, such as pancreatic, breast, colorectal, endometrial and esophageal cancers."

Cancer cells need significantly more glucose than healthy cells to grow and thrive. Restricting carbohydrate intake can significantly limit blood glucose and insulin, a hormone that is released in response to rising blood glucose and that promotes tumor growth in both humans and mice.

In addition to lowering blood glucose levels, a low-carbohydrate, high-protein diet can both boost the immune system's ability to kill cancer cells and prevent obesity.

For the study, Gerald Krystal of the British Columbia Cancer Research Centre and his team implanted various strains of mice with human or mouse cancer cells and assigned them to one of two diets. The first diet, a typical Western diet, contained about 55% carbohydrate (mostly sucrose, or table sugar), 23% protein and 22% fat. The second contained 15% carbohydrate (mostly in the form of starches that were about 70% amylose, a more slowly digested sugar typically found in whole grains, legumes, bananas, sweet potatoes, radishes and parsnips), 58% protein and 26% fat.

The low-carb mice exhibited lower blood-glucose and insulin levels and their tumor cells grew consistently slower than in those fed the high-carbohydrate western diet. They also had lower lactate levels—a chemical that fuels cancer growth and metastasis.

The Many Benefits of a High-Protein, Low-Carb Diet

In addition, mice genetically predisposed to breast cancer were put on the two diets and almost half of those on the Western diet developed breast cancer within their first year of life while none on the low-carbohydrate, high-protein diet did. Only one mouse on the Western diet reached a normal life span (approximately two years), with 70% dying from cancer. Only 30% of those on the low-carbohydrate diet developed cancer and more than half of them reached or exceeded their normal life span.

In addition to lowering blood glucose levels, a low-carbohydrate, high-protein diet can both boost the immune system's ability to kill cancer cells and prevent obesity. "Certain amino acids (i.e., arginine and tryptophan) play a very important role in allowing killer T cells to kill tumor cells," says Krystal.

Moreover, high protein diets lead to more rapid satiety, which reduces obesity. "Obesity has a dramatic effect on cancer incidence, likely, at least in part, by increasing chronic inflammation," he explains.

We should eat some high-quality protein at every meal, but should aim to vary its sources as much as possible.

All this doesn't mean we need to banish carbohydrates forever; however, we need to differentiate between less-healthy carbohydrates that cause a sharp increase in blood glucose and healthier carbs with a gentler glycemic impact.

The former include starchy foods like baked goods made with white flour, potatoes and white rice—all of which make up a large proportion of the calories a typical Westerner eats every day.

Unrefined, Natural Foods Are Best

The latter tend to be unrefined, natural foods such as vegetables, fruits, legumes, nuts or whole grains that are converted more gradually into blood glucose. (Similar to the carbs the healthier mice ate.) These foods also generally contain important anti-cancer plant chemicals; thus they play an important role in an anti-cancer diet. In *Zest for Life* I recommend that people stick to low-glycemic carbohydrates—especially non-starchy vegetables—and eat protein with every meal to keep blood glucose levels stable.

Does increasing protein intake mean eating more meat? Such a conclusion could be problematic, for red and processed meats are thought to increase the risk of colorectal cancer. My view is that we should eat some high-quality protein at every meal, but should aim to vary its sources as much as possible, alternating between fish, white and occasional red meat, eggs, legumes, nuts and minimally processed soy foods; Dr. Krystal uses whey protein isolate powder to boost his protein intake.

It's worth noting that the low-carb, high-protein diet tested in this study is also low in fat (26%, as compared with around 35% in the traditional Mediterranean diet and 50% in the Atkins diet). While hungry, captive mice will eat this kind of diet, humans struggle to stick to low-carb, low-fat diets for long. (A recent survey found that 80% of Dukan dieters regained the weight they had shed on this low-fat, high-protein regimen within three years.)

"It is likely that we could still attain very beneficial effects if we raised the fat slightly and reduced the protein slightly," says Dr. Krystal. Such a diet (say 20% carbohydrate, 40% fat and 40% protein) would also be easier to maintain than the 15% carb, 25% fat and 60% protein model used in the mouse studies, he says.

Again, the ancestral Mediterranean diet may offer the best solution: it is rich in low-glycemic vegetables and fruits, provides plenty of protein through fish, lean meat, legumes and nuts, offers healthy fats in the form of olive, nut and fish oils and is low in sugar and refined grains.

Best of all, it is simple and tasty, making it a pleasure to follow long-term.

Organizations to Contact

The editors have compiled the following list of organizations concerned with the issues debated in this book. The descriptions are derived from materials provided by the organizations. All have publications or information available for interested readers. The list was compiled on the date of publication of the present volume; names, addresses, phone and fax numbers, and e-mail and Internet addresses may change. Be aware that many organizations take several weeks or longer to respond to inquiries, so allow as much time as possible.

American Diabetes Association

1701 North Beauregard St., Alexandria, VA   22311
(800) 342-2383
e-mail: AskADA@diabetes.org
website: www.diabetes.org

The American Diabetes Association funds research to prevent, cure, and manage diabetes. The organization's website includes basic information on diabetes, including descriptions of Type 1 and Type 2 diabetes, symptoms, statistics, common terms, health tips, and myths about diabetes. It also includes information on food, fitness, and lifestyle and how these factors influence the onset of diabetes in people.

American Heart Association (AHA)

7272 Greenville Ave., Dallas, TX   75231
(800) 242-8721
website: www.heart.org

The American Heart Association (AHA) engages in a range of activities, including medical research, professional education, and patient education, to promote a world free of heart disease and stroke. The AHA website provides nutritional guidelines and information on physical activity, stress and weight management, and smoking.

Centers for Disease Control and Prevention (CDC)

1600 Clifton Rd., Atlanta, GA   30333
(800) 232-4636
e-mail: cdcinfo@cdc.gov
website: www.cdc.gov

The Centers for Disease Control and Prevention is a US government agency that focuses on health promotion and the prevention of disease, injury, and disability. The CDC website includes consumer health information on lifestyle diseases, such as heart disease and diabetes, as well as information about food safety and diet.

The Food Industry Center

University of Minnesota, Department of Applied Economics
317 Ruttan Hall, 1994 Buford Ave., St. Paul, MN   55108-6040
(612) 625-7019
e-mail: tfic@umn.edu
website: http://foodindustrycenter.umn.edu

The Food Industry Center at the University of Minnesota, funded by the Alfred P. Sloan Foundation, is a community of scholars and food industry leaders from across the nation and the world. The Center develops and disseminates data and analysis focused on how food moves from farm to fork and how well the industry serves consumers and treats employees.

Urban Farming

19785 West 12 Mile Rd. #537, Southfield, MI   48076
e-mail: info@urbanfarming.org
website: www.urbanfarming.org

Urban Farming educates and organizes inner city communities—sometimes characterized as "food deserts"—to grow their own food, as a way of moving beyond the cycle of poverty and the continual need for emergency food assistance. It also produces educational programs on "green collar jobs" and entrepreneurship, the global economy and emerging industries, and the impact of these developments on food security, health, and nutrition.

US Department of Agriculture, Center for Nutrition Policy and Promotion

3101 Park Center Dr., 10th Floor, Alexandria, VA   22302-1594
(703) 305-7600
website: www.cnpp.usda.gov

The Center for Nutrition Policy and Promotion (CNPP), within the US Department of Agriculture, works to improve the health of Americans by developing and promoting dietary guidance that links scientific research to the nutrition needs of consumers. The agency's website includes considerable information on such topics as nutrition, dietary guidelines, USDA food plans, and other issues.

US Department of Health and Human Services, Health.gov

200 Independence Ave. SW, Washington, DC   20201
(877) 696-6775
website: http://health.gov

The Health.gov website, which publishes current dietary and physical activity guidelines for Americans, is coordinated by the Office of Disease Prevention and Health Promotion, US Department of Health and Human Services. The website evaluates the strength of the evidence supporting each of the guidelines, provides detailed information on the nutrient content of various foods, and also addresses issues like diet-related chronic diseases and food safety.

US National Library of Medicine

Reference and Web Services, 8600 Rockville Pike
Bethesda, MD   20894
(301) 594-5983
website: www.nlm.nih.gov

The US National Library of Medicine (NLM) is the world's largest medical library. The library collects materials and provides information and research services in all areas of biomedicine and health care. The Medline Plus website (www.nlm.nih.gov/medlineplus), produced by NLM, contains consumer health information about diseases, conditions, and wellness issues, written in clear and easily understood language.

Bibliography

Books

Susan Allport   *The Queen of Fats: Why Omega-3s Were Removed from the Western Diet and What We Can Do to Replace Them.* Berkeley: University of California Press, 2006.

Stan Cox   *Sick Planet: Corporate Food and Medicine.* Ann Arbor, MI: Pluto Press, 2008.

Francis Delpeuch   *Globesity: A Planet Out of Control?* Sterling, VA: Earthscan, 2009.

Roberta Larson Duyff   *American Dietetic Association Complete Food and Nutrition Guide.* Hoboken, NJ: John Wiley & Sons, 2006.

David A. Kessler   *The End of Overeating: Taking Control of the Insatiable American Appetite.* Emmaus, PA: Macmillan, 2009.

Barbara Kingsolver   *Animal, Vegetable, Miracle: A Year of Food Life.* New York: Harper Collins Publishers, 2007.

David Kirby   *Animal Factory: The Looming Threat of Industrial Pig, Dairy, and Poultry Farms to Humans and the Environment.* New York: St. Martin's Press, 2010.

Mark Kurlansky   *The Food of a Younger Land.* New York: Riverhead Books, 2009.

Anna Lappé	*Diet for a Hot Planet: The Climate Crisis at the End of Your Fork and What You Can Do About It*. New York: Bloomsbury USA, 2010.
Peter Menzel and Faith D'Aluisio	*What the World Eats*. Berkeley, CA: Tricycle Press, 2008.
Eric Millstone and Tim Lang	*The Atlas of Food*. London: Earthscan, 2008.
Michael Pollan	*In Defense of Food: An Eater's Manifesto*. New York: Penguin Press, 2008.
Michael Pollan	*Food Rules: An Eater's Manual*. New York: Penguin Books, 2009.
Michael Pollan	*The Omnivore's Dilemma: A Natural History of Four Meals*. New York: Penguin Press, 2006.
Eric Schlosser	*Chew on This: Everything You Don't Want to Know About Fast Food*. New York: Houghton Mifflin, 2006.
Eric Schlosser	*Fast Food Nation: The Dark Side of the All-American Meal*. New York: Houghton Mifflin, 2001.
Tom Standage	*An Edible History of Humanity*. New York: Walker & Company, 2009.
Gene Stone, ed.	*Forks Over Knives: The Plant-Based Way to Health*. New York: The Experiment, 2011.

Brian Wansink   *Mindless Eating: Why We Eat More Than We Think.* New York: Bantam Books, 2006.

Karl Weber   *Food, Inc: How Industrial Food Is Making Us Sicker, Fatter and Poorer; and What You Can Do About It: A Participant Guide.* New York: PublicAffairs, 2009.

Periodicals and Internet Sources

Jane E. Brody   "Personal Health; Rules Worth Following, for Everyone's Sake," *New York Times*, February 2, 2010.

Jean-Luc Butel   "How the U.N. Can Undo Damage From Chronic Disease," Fox News.com, November 18, 2011. www.foxnews.com.

Marissa Cevallos   "Chronic Diseases Are a Worldwide Problem," *Los Angeles Times*, April 27, 2011.

Anna Ciezadlo   "Does the Mediterranean Diet Even Exist?," *New York Times*, April 1, 2011.

Nicholas   "White Rice Raises Risk of Type 2
Edmondson   Diabetes, Study Claims," *International Business Times*, March 16, 2012.

Timothy Egan   "Belly Up to the Bistro," *New York Times*, September 15, 2011.

Toni Johnson   "Global Action on
                      Non-Communicable Diseases,"
                      Council on Foreign Relations,
                      September 20, 2011. www.cfr.org.

Kate Kelland   "Chronic Disease to Cost $47 Trillion
                      by 2030: WEF," *Thomson-Reuters
                      AlertNet*, September 18, 2011.
                      www.reuters.com.

N.R. Kleinfield   "Diabetes and Its Awful Toll Quietly
                      Emerge as a Crisis," *New York Times*,
                      January 9, 2006.

Edith M. Lederer   "UN: Deaths Up from Cancer,
                      Diabetes, Heart Disease," *Bloomberg
                      Businessweek*, June 21, 2011.

Jake Marcus   "New Republic: Treating a Silent
                      Global Epidemic," National Public
                      Radio, April 29, 2011. www.npr.org.

Janet Maslin   "Obsessed with Nutrition? That's an
                      Eating Disorder," *New York Times*,
                      January 3, 2008.

*Medical   "More Than 25 Percent of Chinese
News Today*   Adults Are Overweight or Obese;
                      Absent Changes, Rate Expected to
                      Double in 20 Years," July 8, 2008.

Talea Miller   "Diabetes Cases Double, Highest
                      Rates in Oceania and Middle East,"
                      PBS NewsHour, June 27, 2011.
                      www.pbs.org.

William Neuman   "UN Data Notes Sharp Rise in World
                      Food Prices," *New York Times*,
                      January 5, 2011.

Tara Parker-Pope	"Fat Stigma Is Fast Becoming a Global Epidemic," *New York Times*, March 31, 2011.
Kevin Patterson, as told to Terry Gross	"How Western Diets Are Making the World Sick," *Fresh Air*, March 24, 2011. www.npr.org.
Danny Rose	"Inaction on Salt Costing 'A Lot of Lives'," *Sydney Morning Herald*, November 24, 2010.
Gary Taubes	"Is Sugar Toxic?," *New York Times*, April 13, 2011.

Index

A

Acid-base balance, 8
Agribusiness
    health insurers and, 30–31
    production importance in,
      37–38
    promotes lifestyle diseases,
      26–31
    unhealthy food system from,
      32–40
Alcohol use, 7, 20, 21, 22
ALDI grocery store, 58
American Academy of Pediatrics,
  39
American Cancer Society, 46
American diet, 36, 41–43, 71–75
    See also Fast-food diet; Fed-
      eral guidelines on food;
      Food industry; Western diet
American Dietetic Association, 42
*American Journal of Clinical Nutri-
tion* (magazine), 7
American Medical Association
  (AMA), 39, 42
Amino acids, 82
Amylose sugar, 81
Animal rights, 77
Animal Rights Fund, 77
Antibiotic overuse, 33–35, 37–38
Anti-hunger lobby, 69
Arsenic contamination, 33–34

B

Bafna, Dilip, 77
Beef Products, Inc., 33

Berman, Rick, 41–43
Bisphenol A (BPA), 34, 38
Black, Jane, 65–70
Blood glucose levels, 23, 81–83
Blood-estrogen levels, 51
Body mass index, 12
Brazil, 24
Breast cancer
    exercise against, 46, 51
    high-protein, low-carb diet
      and, 82
    treatment against, 48
    US lifestyle and, 45
    vegan diet and, 79
British Columbia Cancer Research
  Centre, 81
British Medical Journal, 41
Bush, George W., 38

C

Cancer
    deaths from, 7
    defined, 47
    glucose and growth of, 80–81
    from high-fat diet, 44
    molecules that affect gene
      activity, 47–49
    risk from obesity, 46, 49–51
    US lifestyle and, 45–46
    vegetarian diet and, 78
    See also specific cancers
Cancer advisory panel, 38
Cancer Research (journal), 80
Carbonated soft drinks, 37
Case Western Reserve University,
  13